GRASS
FORTUNE

LING WANG was born in Nanchang, China, in 1957 and came to Australia in 1990. She currently lives in Melbourne.

GRASS
FORTUNE

My Life Story
LING WANG

PENGUIN BOOKS

Penguin Books

Published by the Penguin Group
Penguin Books Australia Ltd
250 Camberwell Road, Camberwell, Victoria 3124, Australia
Penguin Books Ltd
80 Strand, London WC2R 0RL, England
Penguin Putnam Inc.
375 Hudson Street, New York, New York 10014, USA
Penguin Books Canada Limited
10 Alcorn Avenue, Toronto, Ontario, Canada, M4V 3B2
Penguin Books (N.Z.) Ltd
Cnr Rosedale and Airborne Roads, Albany, Auckland, New Zealand
Penguin Books (South Africa) (Pty) Ltd
24 Sturdee Avenue, Rosebank, Johannesburg 2196, South Africa
Penguin Books India (P) Ltd
11, Community Centre, Panchsheel Park, New Delhi 110 017, India

First published by Penguin Books Australia Ltd 2002

10 9 8 7 6 5 4 3 2 1

Copyright © Ling Wang 2002

The moral right of the author has been asserted

All rights reserved. Without limiting the rights under copyright reserved above, no part of this publication may be reproduced, stored in or introduced into a retrieval system, or transmitted, in any form or by any means (electronic, mechanical, photocopying, recording or otherwise), without the prior written permission of both the copyright owner and the above publisher of this book.

Designed by Brad Maxwell, Penguin Design Studio
Typeset in 10.5/17pt Fairfield Light by Post Pre-press, Brisbane, Queensland
Printed and bound in Australia by McPherson's Printing Group, Maryborough, Victoria

National Library of Australia
Cataloguing-in-Publication data:

Wang, Ling, 1957– .
   Grass fortune: my life story.

   Bibliography.
   Includes index.
   ISBN 0 14 100317 0.

   1. Wang, Ling, 1957– . 2. Women judges – China – Biography.
3. Chinese – Australia – Biography. 4. China – History –
Cultural Revolution, 1966–1976. 5. China – History – 1976– .
1. Title.

347.510234092

 This project has been assisted by the Commonwealth Government through the Australia Council, its arts funding and advisory body.

www.penguin.com.au

To my late grandmother and father
and to my respected mother

ACKNOWLEDGEMENTS

I gratefully acknowledge Helen Cerne at Victoria University of Technology, who has played a huge part in this book. Her encouragement and support gave me the confidence to finish it. I am also extremely grateful to Clare Forster at Penguin and am deeply indebted to my editor Meredith Rose. I thank everyone who contributed, in particular my mother, who generously allowed me to share her stories.

Even a raging fire can not
burn the grass down,
it shoots up again when
the spring breeze blows

Bai Juyi (Tang dynasty)

AUTHOR'S NOTE

The stories in this book are true but most of the names of people, other than my family, have been changed. In accordance with Chinese custom, the names of some younger people are preceded with the affectionate *Xiao*, and some older people with the respectful *Lao*. A person's family name precedes their given name, so that in China I am known as Wang Ling.

CONTENTS

出生逸事	Birth 1
童年时光	Childhood 9
茁壮成长	Adolescence 22
待业青年	Job-Waiting Youth 34
坎坷之路	Twists and Turns 42
父业熏陶	Father 57
一波三折	Endless Setbacks 79
初到法院	The First Task 94
死刑执行	The Execution 106
法权较量	Between Power and Law 116
进退两难	In a Dilemma 139
不畏压力	Under Pressure 155
单身烦恼	The Vexation of Being Single 175
是赢是输	Win or Lose 193
面对干扰	Facing Interference 208
外国原告	The Foreign Plaintiff 228
双重麻烦	Double Trouble 244
人生转折	A Dramatic Turn 264
告别过去	Say Goodbye to the Past 278

出 生 逸 事
BIRTH

I was an unexpected girl for my family.

My parents already had a daughter, and as they planned to have only two children they wanted a boy for their second child. My father wanted a son to play chess with and go fishing with. My mother hoped to bear my father a male heir because she didn't want to hear her husband blamed for not continuing his ancestry. According to traditional Chinese thought, people had children in order to carry on their family lines, and only sons were able to do this. A couple needed to have at least one son, otherwise the family line would be discontinued and this was disrespectful to the ancestors. The wife might even be thrown out as punishment. Although such punitive actions are no longer taken in modern China, this way of thinking is still entrenched in people's minds. Even today, people think having a son is glorious.

My grandmother, who lived with my parents, also hoped for a grandson. She had no son herself, only two daughters – my mother was her second child. My grandfather had been a connoisseur of curios and a man of property. He had run a big company. Unfortunately he died when my mother was only eleven months old. In the old China, few women could run a business and only sons could inherit their fathers' companies, so as soon as my grandfather died, other directors took over the business and asked my grandmother to sign a declaration. She did not know what was written on it as she could read just a few words, and only later did she realise that she had lost all the property that should have belonged to her. After that she became a poor widow and had to live by her two hands. She brought her daughters up by doing hard work, such as cooking, washing and cleaning. My grandmother always said that if she had had a son she would not have had such a hard life.

When my mother became pregnant for the second time in the summer of 1956, my grandmother tried every means to find out if she was going to have a grandson. At that time, of course, there was no such thing as an ultrasound to indicate a baby's sex. (And even in present-day China, people are prevented from using these tests to find out their baby's gender in case they abort their foetus on discovering it to be a girl. China has an official policy of allowing one child per family, and many people still want that child to be a son, not a daughter.) My grandmother went to see a blind fortune-teller. After asking a few questions about my mother and her pregnancy, the fortune-teller lowered his head, extended his right hand and calculated on his fingers. After a while, he raised his head and smiled at my grandmother. 'Congratulations! You will have a grandson soon.' My grandmother was so pleased to hear this news, she paid him double the money and gave him her many thanks.

A few days later, my grandmother learnt from a friend another method for predicting the baby's gender. She asked my mother to take out some rice from the rice bucket and explained, 'It's said the pregnant woman will bear a boy if the number of grains she takes out is an odd number, and she will bear a girl if it is an even number.' Compliant with her mother's words, my mother closed her eyes, took out some rice using three fingers, and placed the grains on the table. My grandmother put on her glasses and counted them one by one, very carefully. 'One, two, three . . . seven . . . ten . . . thirteen grains. It's an odd number!' She was overjoyed.

'It's fourteen. There is a little one.' The words of the housekeeper, Lao Chen, stopped my grandmother's laughter.

'Nonsense! It's less than half. It can't be taken as a grain.' My grandmother was angry with Chen.

'Yes, you're right. Round up or down. This small one can't be taken as a grain.' Chen, recognising she had made a slip of the tongue, hastened to amend it.

Although my family believed a boy was coming to our home, one thing still made my grandmother feel uneasy. There is a proverb in China which says, 'Sour boy, hot girl.' It means a pregnant woman will bear a boy if she likes to eat sour food, and a girl if she likes to eat hot food. My mother liked both sour and hot – this made my grandmother very confused and worried. One day, with her friend's help, she brought an old country woman to see my mother. It was said this woman could tell a baby's sex by feeling the mother's pulse. The woman asked my mother to extend an arm and lay it on the table. She put her four fingers on my mother's wrist. A few minutes later, she said seriously, 'It's a boy, definitely.' My grandmother and my mother smiled from ear to ear when they heard this.

From that day, my grandmother was convinced that a boy was going to join the family. She asked my father to buy pictures of chubby boys and she put them up on the wall of every room. She had my mother send my sister's old clothes to others and buy some pieces of beautiful new cloth. In the evenings, the only thing my grandmother did was make clothing for the coming boy. Soon, a few sets of clothes, hats, pairs of socks and shoes had been prepared for a male child.

My family lived in an apartment on the third floor of a four-storey block in Nanchang, the capital of Jiangxi province in southern China. Four other families lived on the same floor, and next door was a young couple. The wife, Xiao Liu, was also pregnant. Sharing a kitchen, the two families had many opportunities to be together, and had been getting on very well. My mother and Xiao Liu were good friends and discussed all kinds of matters with each other. Both being pregnant, they had much in common. One day, my mother was talking to Xiao Liu in the kitchen when my grandmother called her to come back. My mother didn't know why her mother was displeased. My grandmother said in a serious tone, 'From now on, don't get closer to Xiao Liu. She's also pregnant. It's said the foetus can be changed if pregnant women often get together. I don't know if it's true, but just in case . . . ' My mother respected her wishes and never talked to Xiao Liu again.

The spring of 1957 was coming and the weather was getting warmer and warmer. Leaves turned green and all kinds of flowers were sending out buds. The expected date of my birth was also approaching. When my mother was almost due, the whole family started to get nervous as my sister Ping's birth had involved a difficult labour. My father could still remember the doctor's question: 'Who do you want to protect first, your wife or your baby?' What a curly question! How hard to choose! My father had thrown the difficulty back to the doctor. 'I want both my wife and my baby safe.' Fortunately this proved to be the case.

My grandmother, however, had one more worry. She was afraid her grandson had been changed into a girl and she went to the temple almost every morning to ask the bodhisattva to bless her daughter and her grandson.

At the end of April, on a quiet, dark morning when people were still sound asleep, my mother suddenly felt labour pains. She woke up my father. 'Quick! Send me to the hospital.' My father rushed down from the third floor to the ground floor and knocked at the door of Wu Jian, the driver of my father's work unit, to ask him to drive them to the hospital, then made a phone call to the hospital to let them know they were coming.

Half an hour later, Wu Jian stopped the car in front of the main building of the Women's and Children's Hospital in Nanchang. A doctor and two nurses were waiting at the door and they ran to the car with a stretcher.

'Hurry up! Send the patient to the delivery room straight away,' the doctor ordered.

But there was no time, my mother was in the advanced stage of labour. The doctor climbed into the car. 'Pass me the sheet,' she called.

A white sheet was put on the back seat of the car where my mother was lying. The two nurses got into the car from each side. Very soon, it was my cry that was heard instead of my mother's. So I, an unexpected girl born hurriedly in a car, joined a family who wanted a boy.

My mother's pale face appeared a little disappointed when she heard I was a girl. My grandmother said persistently that the foetus had been changed and was so upset that she refused to smile even when relatives and friends came to say congratulations. A friend of my mother's said with good intentions, 'This is the Year of the Chicken, it is good that she was born in the morning. The crowing of roosters heralds the break of day.' Hearing this, my grandmother was not appreciative and said, 'Only cocks can herald the break of day, hens only lay eggs.' But my father was delighted as a child with my birth.

After I had been shown to my family, I was put in the nursery and taken to my mother five times a day. The baby carriage of the hospital was one and a half metres in length and just over half a metre wide. Babies were put crosswise in it, but I was so long I could not fit like the other babies, and every time the newborn were sent to their mothers for feeding, the nurse had to hold me while she pushed the carriage with her other hand. The other mothers were not happy, complaining that the nurse favoured me, but when they were shown that I was too long to fit, my mother won the admiration of the other mothers because of my size.

Soon I grew bigger and bigger, fatter and fatter. I was also quiet and seldom cried. My mother quickly forgot her disappointment and looked after me lovingly, but my grandmother still did not accept me and almost never even glanced at me. When I was about four months old I found my thumbs were delicious. Lying in my cradle, in the daytime or awake at midnight, I always put them into my mouth, sucking with great relish. And it was because of this habit that I finally won my grandmother's affection.

One day, my grandmother and my parents were having lunch at the table. As usual, I was sucking my thumb, often making clicking noises. My grandmother left the table and walked toward me. She stood beside the cradle watching me for a while, then she couldn't help smiling and said, 'She looks very lovely!' Her line of sight remained on my hair. Though my face took after my father's, my thick black hair was straight and stiff and didn't look like his naturally wavy locks. My grandmother took all my hair and joined it together until it stood up straight on my head. It was over two inches high.

'It's very strange! It looks like a cockscomb,' Lao Chen shouted.

'How can you say it is like a cockscomb? It should be called a phoenix's comb,' my grandmother corrected her. The phoenix is a sacred bird in ancient Chinese legend, symbolising luck and happiness. My grandmother turned to my parents. 'I don't mind her formal name being Ling, but at home I think

Feng Er is more suitable for her.' Feng is the Chinese word for phoenix, and Er is a pet name used for children.

After that, everybody called me Feng Er, until my hair could no longer stand up.

童年时光
CHILDHOOD

The year I was born was an unforgettable one for Chinese people. In the early summer of 1957 Mao Zedong launched the Anti-Rightist Campaign. The criterion for being labelled a rightist was having an opinion considered to run counter to the Communist Party, the dictatorship of the proletariat, or the socialist system. In every work unit – government organisations, schools, universities, and so on – an anti-rightist group was set up. These groups encouraged people to expose each other's rightist words and deeds and then ranged them in order of seriousness, labelling people as rightists down the list until the quota was filled.

Over five hundred thousand people were labelled as rightists because they had criticised the Party's policies, complained about the system, voiced a differing political opinion, expressed their discontent with their work leaders, or because they had an unsuitable class background. Some people were branded as rightists simply because the quota had not been met. Everyone was affected, including cadres, scientists, teachers and students.

My family did not avoid disaster. At that time, my father

had a leading position in an important section of government. After serving in the army from 1947 to 1951, he had been transferred to the Supervisory Committee of the Jiangxi Provincial Industrial Bureau, where his job was to oversee matters relating to productivity control, finance, workers' compensation, personnel, and so on, in a large number of factories. One day, the head of the anti-rightist group in the Industrial Bureau came to interrogate my father about a work colleague named Hu, who had just graduated from university and was five years younger than my father.

'Someone has reported that Hu said many offensive things about our Party in a conversation with you,' said the head of the anti-rightist group, a middle-aged woman. 'You are an old revolutionary and have had the benefit of the Party's education for many years. We hope you will reveal these reactionary opinions as a witness.'

My father was resentful. 'In my memory, Hu didn't say any reactionary words. You'd better ask whoever reported that to be the witness.'

'Then you're concealing his mistakes on purpose. You should know the cost for this,' the woman warned.

'I don't think I need to conceal anything about him.' My father hated to be threatened. 'He didn't say anything against the Party, he only made some comments about a leader of our unit. You can do whatever you want to me. I don't care.'

One month later, Hu had been labelled as a rightist and, as happened to all rightists, he was sacked from his position and sent to a farm to be reformed through labour. He remained in the countryside for thirty years, until his grievance was redressed. By then government policy had changed; his rightist label was revoked and he was allowed to return to the city. My father was very sad that he had not been able to protect such an honest and promising young man, but as it turned out he was unable to protect even himself. Liao Hongyi, the work-unit leader Hu had been critical of, was angry about my father's attitude and said he must have right-deviationist thoughts himself since he had protected Hu. Because the rightist quota for my father's unit was already full, he received only a light punishment and was demoted by three ranks. But in November of that year he was given a similar punishment to the rightists, even though he still had not been labelled as such, and was assigned to the mountainous region of Wugong to discipline himself through manual labour. The only difference was that he still received a salary – even though it was cut – whereas most rightists received only a living allowance.

It was very common at that time for unit leaders to use campaigns in order to revenge personal grudges, as Liao had done. Feigning concern for my family's needs, he wrote to my mother's work unit suggesting it assign her to accompany my father, and her name too was added to the list for Wugong, which was more than a hundred kilometres from Nanchang.

'You have just been approved as a Party member,' my mother's work-unit leader told her, 'and we need you to set a good example in following the Party's orders. What's more, there's an allowance for you and you'll get to live with your husband.'

My mother, who had graduated from Beijing's Central Institute for Commerce, worked as an accountant in the Jiangxi Provincial Commercial Bureau while my grandmother looked after my sister and me. She told her leader that she did not want to go. 'I don't believe this is being done out of concern for me,' my mother said. 'You're giving me tight shoes to wear, making things hard for me by abusing your power.'

'It's up to you,' the leader warned angrily. 'If you go, you can stay a Party member; if not, the approval will be revoked. Of course, you have another choice, which is to divorce your husband.'

In early December, one week after my father had left, my mother went to ask for help from the ministry in charge of her work unit. Ho was the Minister of the Financial and Trading Ministry and was a good, kind man. He intervened and had the decision overturned, so that my mother avoided going to the mountains after all. But her Party membership was annulled and we lived in Nanchang without my father for four years.

I was seven months old when my father was sent to Wugong, and my first memory of him is as a three-year-old when he came back home for a holiday. I recall him being very tall, thin and handsome, with naturally curly hair. He held me up over his head again and again, and then put me on his knee, cuddling me in his arms with his face nestled up against mine. I could feel his love for me. Unfortunately I enjoyed such paternal love only once a year, all the leave that was allowed under government policy, and even then my father had to apply for permission from the head of the labour camp.

In July 1960 my mother gave birth to my sister Jing. My father had been allowed home for the occasion and one day, when he set off to the shops on his bicycle, I followed him without anyone noticing. The shop was not too far away and there were not many people on the road. I could see my father's back in the distance but I still lost him. When I reached the shop I couldn't find him anywhere. I went inside and called for him in a low voice until an old woman asked me who I was looking for. I told her but I didn't know where I lived. Taking me by the hand, she led me out of the shop and told me to stand right there, where it would be easier for my father to notice me. Nearly two hours later, he did find me, still standing there with the old woman and with an ice-pop in my hand. He had looked for me everywhere before thinking of the shop. Holding me tightly, he kissed my cheeks over and over.

Years later, I discovered that my disappearance had given my mother a great shock, while my grandmother, once again disappointed by the birth of a girl, had blamed my new sister for this adversity.

Then, in late 1961, came the wonderful news that my father would be returning to Nanchang permanently. The reason for his return was not so wonderful – he had sustained a severe chest injury during disciplinary labour – but thankfully he was all right. He had been working in a group moving cut trees down to the foot of a hill, and after several hours of this heavy work everyone was tired. My father was carrying a thick trunk with another man, struggling with it down a rugged path, when suddenly the other man stumbled. The tree fell on my father's chest and as a result of his injury he had difficulty breathing, a constant cough and pain. The doctor declared that it would take a long time to heal, and as my father was unable to engage in heavy labour any more, he was allowed to come home. He did not return to his old job but was transferred to the Nanchang People's Bank, whose head had served in the army with my father and now invited him to work with him.

That was a time of great natural calamity in China and many people died of hunger. Droughts and flood had destroyed most of the crops and food was scarce. Luckily, my father had a friend who was the director of the Nanchang Non-Staple Food Company and he managed to give us a hundred kilos of cabbage and some tinned fish. My sisters and I ate these at every meal but my parents did not touch even a small piece of fish. All they had was a bowl of porridge with cabbage, and soon they suffered from dropsy in their faces and legs.

In September of that year I had started kindergarten. Every day I studied, played, sang and danced. I was keen on reading and when I came home I spent hours reading picture books from the street library. I also collected my elder sister Ping's old Chinese and maths textbooks and learnt them page by page. I asked my parents and Ping endless questions. In China, children in Grade One at primary school have to learn to read and write more than a hundred characters, and be proficient in addition, subtraction and simple division. By the time I left kindergarten, I had already finished the textbooks for Grade

Three. After my selection examination, I was enrolled at Zhu Shi Primary School, one of the top three in Nanchang, and was put straight into Grade Two. Every term I was given the award of *san hao xuesheng* – students who were good in quality, study and health – and became the darling of my parents and teachers. I was simple and unaffected, free from all anxieties. I felt I was the happiest girl in the world.

But my happiness was not to last long. In the summer of 1966, when I had nearly finished my study in Grade Three, Mao Zedong launched the Great Proletarian Cultural Revolution and my life was suddenly thrown into upheaval.

Mao claimed that, even though China had undergone a political revolution in 1949 when the Communist Party came to power, a cultural revolution was needed in order to root out the old thoughts, culture and customs that still remained in people's minds. Initially, the domain of culture was the most important front for this continuous revolution, with many literary works, songs, plays and films being labelled as 'big poisonous weeds' and banned. But soon the Cultural Revolution expanded to all aspects of society, with catchphrases like 'capitalist revisionist', 'distortion of Marxism-Leninism', 'down with feudalism' and 'capitalist-roader' heard everywhere. A great number of people, both leaders and non-leaders, who had unsuitable class backgrounds were criticised and removed from their offices. As happened during the Anti-Rightist Campaign, having parents with the wrong class background was enough to get you labelled a counter-revolutionary, and many people were sent to labour camps to be re-educated.

One year later, the Cultural Revolution moved into its second stage, with the population falling naturally into two camps – the rebels, who supported the movement, and the loyalists, who did not. While no one dared to openly oppose the Cultural Revolution, the loyalists still secretly supported the old leaders. The struggle between the two groups quickly descended into violence, fuelled by posters exhorting people to uphold the class struggle. Countless people were killed and injured, with the first person to die in the violence in Nanchang being a schoolgirl just thirteen years old. The whole country was thrown into confusion. Factories, government offices, schools and universities were all closed; nobody was working and nobody was studying. Everyone was expected to participate in the revolution, including old people and children, and this state of chaos lasted until 1968.

There were no longer any formal classes at my school, only praise for Chairman Mao and the Communist Party through song and dance. As I enjoyed singing and dancing, I was still immersed in happiness, until one day my teacher, who liked me very much, pulled me aside from the final rehearsal for a performance. Her solemn face made me feel strange and frightened.

'You can't go on with dance,' she told me. 'Because of your father's political problem, you have to attend the study group for the *hei jiu lei zi nu* (the children of the nine kinds of 'black' people: landlords, rich peasants, counter-revolutionaries, evildoers, rightists, traitors, spies, power-holders and intellectuals).

You'd better make a clean break with him.' The teacher also said something else that I didn't understand – I didn't even hear her at all, I just watched my classmates who were dancing merrily. I only knew I couldn't dance among them any longer and I burst into tears.

I did not believe my father was a bad man. I wanted to ask him what had happened. Choking back my tears, I went to his office. When I got close to his building, I saw my father standing in front of it with another two people. A big board was hung around his neck. His head was lowered and his face had no expression. I was shocked. I threw myself at him and held his arm, and could not help crying.

'Father, what's going on? Why are you here like this? You're not bad, are you?'

'Baby, don't cry. Believe your father. I'll always be your good father.' From his eyes, I saw his heart was bleeding.

'Go back home. Don't tell your mother,' he urged me. I swept away my tears and promised not to say anything.

During dinner, my father talked to my mother and played with my sisters and me as if nothing had happened. Watching his haggard face, I felt a twinge in my nose, like I was going to cry. I didn't want my mother to be aware of it as she would be upset, but actually she knew everything already. She understood my father had not said a word about his situation to her because he didn't want her worrying about him, so she pretended to know nothing in order to keep a relaxed atmosphere at home.

One rainy afternoon a few days later, my father was all wet when he came back home.

'It's too cruel! How could they let you stand in the rain?' my mother could not help saying when she dried him. 'I think you have a fever.'

'You know everything?' my father asked.

My mother did not answer him but checked his temperature. 'It's 39.6°. You can't go tomorrow.'

'No, I must. They won't agree to that.'

'I'll go and have it out with them.' She was angry and raised her voice.

'Sshh! Don't let your mother know. She will be upset.'

But my grandmother had heard them talking. 'You stay at home tomorrow,' she said. 'I don't believe they will dare to pull you out from home.' She was also greatly distressed.

At nine the next morning, as my father lay in bed with a high fever and a headache, four people from his work unit forced their way into our apartment.

'Where is he hiding? Get out!' they shouted to us as they checked every room.

When they found my father still sleeping, they howled at him, 'Get up quickly! Don't make us drag you out!'

'He has had a high temperature all night. Let him have a rest today, please,' my mother protested, indicating my father who could hardly get up.

'Don't feign death! Be quick!'

'Get out of here, all of you! Otherwise I won't be so easy on you,' shouted my grandmother, who came up to warn them with a long wooden broomstick in her hand.

'Do you dare to hurt us?'

'Why not? As long as you dare to touch my son-in-law.' She raised the broom and waved it at them. 'I'm of working-class origin. You won't dare to take me away.'

In those days, people who were of a 'good', lower socio-economic class seemed to have the right to do anything they wanted. The men gave up on my father and left, afraid my grandmother would beat them.

But that afternoon we found a big-character poster on the wall of our apartment building, criticising my father's bad attitude to the masses' dictatorship. (Big-character posters had first appeared at the start of the Cultural Revolution and quickly became weapons with which to publicly attack people.) A banner about a metre wide and ten metres long had also been put up on the wall, stretching from one side of the house to the other, and sealing our front door. It read: DOWN WITH THE POWER-HOLDERS! DOWN WITH LANDLORDS, RICH PEASANTS, COUNTER-REVOLUTIONARIES, EVILDOERS AND RIGHTISTS!

It was an unbearable insult. Without telling my parents, I tore down the poster and banner. I felt so proud afterwards – I suddenly understood how to distinguish good and bad, true and false, fair and unfair, love and hatred. I swore that I would severely punish those bad people on behalf of my father when I grew up.

But my mother was alarmed and told me not to do such a thing again. 'It will only bring your father more trouble,' she told me. My father patted me on the head and said, 'You're only a child. Don't get involved in adult affairs.'

In the middle of the night two weeks later, a hubbub awoke me. I got up to find some strange people sitting in the living room. My father was talking with a short, middle-aged man with a black face. My mother and grandmother were whispering in the kitchen.

'How can we protect this bad man and his family?' my grandmother said. 'Let me throw them out.'

'No, we can't do that. They are in danger. His workers are waiting for them outside in the yard,' my mother argued persuasively.

'That's not our business. Have you forgotten it was him who brought disaster to our family?'

'No, I'll remember it all my life. But –'

'What disaster do you mean?' I couldn't help walking in and asking.

My grandmother was startled at my sudden appearance. 'Ten years ago,' she told me, 'it was this man who, in order to settle a personal grudge, reduced your father's rank and sent him to a labour camp in the mountains, scattering our family for four years. Your father is still suffering because of this.'

I rushed into the living room where the revengeful Liao Hongyi was sitting with his wife and two children. I said loudly, 'You have already done great harm to my father and now you want to make more trouble for our family. All of you, get out of here immediately! Or I will let those people in.' I turned and ran downstairs. Our apartment block was in a big yard with five other buildings. There was a security guard who did not allow strangers in unless they could give the name of the person they wished to visit. I ran quickly to the gate, where dozens of people thronged. They held wooden rods and other weapons and shouted, 'Down with Liao Hongyi! Liao Hongyi get out!'

It was obvious that Liao would be attacked if he appeared before these angry people. I stopped, hesitating, and imagined Liao down on the ground, his whole body covered in blood. Just then, I heard my mother calling me.

'Ling! Come back!' She caught up with me and pulled me away from the gate. Turning me to face her, she said, 'Look, it's true Liao did bad things to us. He was wrong to do them, but we can't drop stones on someone who's fallen into the well.' She took me inside.

I went back to bed but could not fall asleep. The next day, I learnt that the angry group at the gate had finally dispersed. Liao and his family stayed with us for a few days, before leaving to return to his hometown. I did not understand my parents' behaviour until many years later, when I finally realised that forgiveness is a virtue.

茁 壮 成 长

ADOLESCENCE

By late 1968 the Cultural Revolution was in its last stage. The central government, seeing that the whole situation was getting out of hand, had issued a series of commands to stop the violence, recover production and resume study. Mao Zedong sent out a directive calling on all young people and cadres to go to the countryside to be re-educated by the peasants. By the end of that year, schools had reopened and the worst excesses of the Cultural Revolution were over, although no one officially announced that it had ended until Jiang Qing (Mao's wife) and her Gang of Four were eradicated in 1976.

Large numbers of people had been sent to rural areas, including cadres in government departments, students from universities and high schools, teachers, doctors and actors. The Public Security Bureau – the Chinese equivalent of the police force – along with the Public Prosecution Organ and the law courts, the three institutions responsible for the execution of law and order in China, were all smashed, as they were seen as instruments of the bourgeois dictatorship. The majority of police officers, prosecutors and judges were sent to the countryside and the whole legal system was paralysed.

This time my family could not escape going to the countryside. My father was assigned to Jin An county, more than a hundred and fifty kilometres from Nanchang, while my mother was assigned to a different county a hundred kilometres from Jin An. My family faced being split in two. Once again my mother had to seek help, this time from the vice-director of the Provisional Revolutionary Committee, who had been a leader in my mother's work unit and had appreciated her moral qualities and work capability. At my mother's request he wrote to the governor of the town of Liantang, and my whole family was able to go there instead. My mother had chosen Liantang because it was my grandmother's home town and was closer to Nanchang, just twenty kilometres away.

In December 1968 everyone except my elder sister Ping was moved in two trucks to a village near the town of Liantang. Ping's entire high school had been transferred to a farm fifty kilometres away and she had to go with it. She lived at the farm and spent half her time studying, including political study, and half her time doing manual labour. My father was put in charge of the medical centre in Liantang and my mother was in charge of the propaganda section.

The village where we lived faced east. There was a big pond in front of it where every morning the sun rose as if a red ball were jumping out of the water. Along the banks grew many poplars and weeping willows. At the back of the village were hills covered in big pine trees. There were sixty-two families living in this little village. The leader was an old man of around sixty; he was not tall and was slightly hunchbacked, but he was a kind man. He brought some cadres to meet my family at the gate of the village and arranged for us to live in the biggest and most beautiful house, which had belonged to a landlord. The house had four bedrooms and a huge living room with a decorated carved door opening out to a small yard paved with red stones. There was a portrait of Mao Zedong on the wall facing the door. A vertically pasted scroll of calligraphy hung on each side of the portrait. 'Follow Mao Zedong' was written on the scroll to the right, and 'Make revolution forever' on that to the left. The village leader told us this was a *zhong zi tai* expressing the village's loyalty to the great leader Chairman Mao.

As soon as we were settled in our new home, Jing and I went to primary school. According to my age, I was placed in Grade Six, though I had stopped studying at school when I was in Grade Three, once the Cultural Revolution had begun. The teachers and students were very friendly to me and I was doubly excited because of moving to a new place and entering a new school. Only one thing made me unhappy – I was expected to go to sleep at seven-thirty every night when, in order to save power, the village turned off all the lights. The whole village became pitch-black at that time, and on the first evening no one in my family could fall asleep. We just talked in the dark. The next day, my father bought a kerosene lamp from a shop in the village so that I could go on reading in the dim light for another two hours after the power was turned off.

Our living and study conditions were hard but they didn't affect my education as I enjoyed learning. I quickly adapted myself to these circumstances and I didn't notice at all how my parents worried about their children's future. During that time in China, there was a big difference between conditions in urban and rural areas. Peasants had the hardest lives and their children generally remained peasants, generation after generation. They had very little resources through which to leave their rural lifestyle. My parents worried that we sisters would become peasants too, as they did not know when or whether they would be able to return to the city.

About two months after we moved to the village, my father received a telegram from his brother saying their mother had died. My father wanted to go home to Shenyang for a viewing of the body. He had been his mother's favourite son. When he joined the army in 1947 she missed him so much that she cried every day. Soon her eyes deteriorated and she began to lose her sight. My father had returned home from the army in 1952 and that was the last time he had seen her. Train travel was expensive and while my family did not have a bad life, it was never possible to save much. Of course, my father's political troubles had not made it easy for him to visit his mother either.

Shenyang, in Liaoning province in China's north-east, was a three-day train journey away. The return ticket was more than a hundred yuan, as much as my parents' joint monthly income. After covering living expenses, there was little left over, so that afternoon my mother went to a second-hand shop in Liantang and sold her watch for a hundred and twenty yuan. The watch had been a wedding gift from my father and was the most valuable thing in our family. In the evening my mother handed my father five hundred and twenty yuan, all their savings plus the money she'd got for her watch.

'Go and buy a train ticket tomorrow and take part in the funeral,' she said.

My father knew at once what she had done. He said nothing but he couldn't hide his tears. This was the first time I had seen him cry.

Early next morning, my father went into Liantang. When he came back, my mother asked if he had bought the ticket. He shook his head and handed her her watch.

'I have decided not to go,' he said. 'My mother has died already. I'd rather send some money back than spend it on my travelling expenses. The funeral will cost money.'

'You shouldn't have got the watch back or you could have sent more.'

'I've sent five hundred. I sold my watch.'

Both my father and mother were very upset, not only because his mother was dead, but also because of the hard situation they were in. They felt pessimistic about their gloomy prospects and feared that the days ahead would be even harder. They placed all their hopes on their daughters, encouraging us to value our time and to study hard.

One year later, I turned thirteen. I graduated from primary school and went to Liantang High School. It was a long way there and took me forty minutes by foot. I walked this four times a day. Every day I left home at six-forty and got to school at seven-thirty for the morning reading. Every day we read Chairman Mao's works – this was more important than any other course and nobody was allowed to be late. I would go back home for lunch at midday, have half an hour at home, and after a hurried meal return to school at two, leaving again at five.

For half of the four kilometres to school, I walked alongside a river. Being a small town, Liantang was very different to Nanchang and I didn't pass any houses, only fields and trees. But I could see the houses of the village and the hills in the distance. When the weather was bad, and especially before a storm, the wind would blow up off the surface of the river. Black clouds would engulf everything, and the grey sky connected with the grey river, as if the whole world were water. On rainy days I couldn't take an umbrella, in case it was swept away by the wind, and me along with it.

But the most difficult thing about getting to school for me was that, according to the rule of the school, every time I went there I had to carry a spade and two square-bottomed bamboo baskets of fertiliser on a shoulder pole. All the other students were from local peasants' families and had their own vegetable gardens, so they could easily take fertiliser from home. My family had no vegetable garden, so I had to find the fertiliser myself. Actually, I didn't even know what fertiliser was. I just shovelled some dark-coloured soil into the baskets on my way to school, but I didn't fill them as full as the other students did; usually my baskets held only about fifteen kilos.

One afternoon, I left home without finishing my lunch as I had to hurry to find fertiliser. It seemed that all the dark-coloured soil on the way had been taken away by me. Finally I had to shovel some soil with grass in it from under some big trees. When I put the baskets down in the corridor at school and was about to enter the classroom, I heard Lao Qin, the director of the grade, praising two girls who were always late but always carried two full baskets of fertiliser into the classroom. It was obvious to me that they did that for the purpose of showing everybody how hard they had worked.

'Why are you late? Where is your fertiliser?' Lao Qin stopped praising and turned to ask when he saw me. He was a middle-aged man, cold-faced and bare-headed. His eyes were small but very sharp. He stressed physical labour, saying that it was the first priority and study the second. He liked those students who were strong and worked actively. He didn't like students who were weak like me, and he thought the reason why I was not strong was that I didn't do enough physical work.

I didn't answer his questions, but carried my baskets in and showed him.

'Have a look at the others' baskets.' Lao Qin pointed to the two girls' baskets. 'And then have a look at yours. You have only brought half of theirs.'

I had done my best. Fifteen kilos was quite a heavy load for me. I felt wronged when I thought of my red and swollen shoulders, but I didn't want to explain anything. After that, the comment I always obtained in my school report was, 'This student has got excellent results in study, but needs to discipline herself through physical labour.'

The education system of the high school was different from primary school. We only had four classes in the morning and every class began with the teacher saying, 'Please take out *The Quotations of Chairman Mao* and turn to page . . .' When the students were ready, the teacher would continue, 'Please read aloud paragraph two. Chairman Mao teaches us . . .' We students would go on reading the paragraph, then the teacher started the lecture.

During the three hours in the afternoon, we did physical labour. Outside the school ground, there was a huge piece of land divided into small plots and assigned separately to each class. My class had forty-two students and the land for which we were responsible was more than two thousand square metres. We grew peanuts and sweet potatoes and some other plants. There was a Peasants' Propaganda Team in the school which was in charge of carrying out the policy that 'Students should learn from workers, learn from peasants and learn from soldiers.' As our school was located in the countryside, we only learnt from peasants. The Peasants' Propaganda Team was composed of dozens of peasants from nearby villages. Each class had a peasant as an instructor and we learnt to do such things as loosening the soil, watering, hoeing and fertilising.

I felt more and more tired after labouring every day and was getting thinner and weaker, which made my parents' hearts ache. They persuaded me from studying in the evening as they were more worried about my health than my study. As they worried, I became sick at last.

September the first was the first day of my second year of study in high school. Soon after lunch we were asked to labour on a peanut plot. We started with the watering, a difficult job because there was no water pipe nearby. We had to go down the hill with plastic basins to fetch water from a small river, and carry the full basins back up to sprinkle water on the plot, doing this again and again. I lost count of how many times later it was when I felt my legs shaking as I walked up the hill with the water. My throat felt parched and my heart was beating fast. I had to sit down on the bank of the plot to have a rest for a while. As soon as I rested, I saw Lao Qin walking toward us. I hurried to stand up and go on carrying the water, but as soon as I stood up I felt dizzy and everything went dark.

This was the first time I had ever fainted. Usually, with such dizzy spells, I recovered after I closed my eyes and stood still for a few minutes. This time I couldn't stand still because Lao Qin was coming, and I didn't want him to see me and criticise me for being weak. So I pretended nothing was wrong and turned down the hill path, though I couldn't see my way at all. Later, my classmates told me that I suddenly fell down after I turned around. They were all scared. I woke up soon after in Liantang hospital feeling very dizzy and weak. I felt sorry when I saw my classmates around me with worried eyes, but I quickly sat up in the bed when I saw Lao Qin standing at the back. The doctor pushed me back down gently and said, 'Don't move. You are on an intravenous drip.'

I persisted in getting up. 'I can't lie here. I must go to work,' I said.

'No, you can't. I have told your director that you are suffering serious anaemia. You can't attend heavy physical work or mental work until your situation gets better. You need rest and nutrition at the moment.' The doctor pushed me down again.

Complying with the doctor's advice, I didn't go to school but stayed at home where my grandmother cooked many delicious and nutritious dishes for me. She would put an egg in a small bowl, stir it well, then pour in boiling water. Covering the bowl, she would leave it for five minutes and then add some sugar. If eaten every day, this mixture was good for curing dizziness and headaches. To make a soup that was also good for headaches, she placed a root herb and some walnuts in cold water and stewed them slowly for a few hours before adding salt. And to treat anaemia she made a soup of peanuts, red beans, red Chinese dates and sugar. Along with these things, my grandmother fed me chicken and pork and I also took several kinds of traditional medicine twice a day. I seemed to be eating all day long.

For the first few days I hated to be at home but soon it felt easy. I found I had more time to study than at school. I made a self-study plan and a timetable. Every morning, after breakfast and medicine, I studied mathematics, then physics. After lunch I spent only one hour on English because the texts were simple and related to political education. There were slogans such as 'Long live Chairman Mao and the Communist Party of China'; 'We shall never forget the class struggle'; 'Pay special attention to the revolution and promote production'. The grammar involved was also easy. The rest of the time I concentrated on Chinese, especially reading and composition. Besides my diary, I enjoyed poetry writing and I wrote a short poem almost every day. The topics I chose included sunshine, flowers, snow, seasons, landscape and activities. My grandmother was my first and most faithful audience. I read each poem to her as she couldn't read herself:

ODE TO THE PLUM BLOSSOM

Don't say all flowers have disappeared when winter comes.
There is a sole spray still sending forth a delicate fragrance.
She aspires to dissolve her pure and noble body in the snow,
And let others contend for glamour in spring and autumn.

'Good, good!' My grandmother always looked as if she really enjoyed my poems and she kept encouraging me. 'Keep studying and practising. What you have learnt must be used some day in the future.' I held her words in my mind though I didn't yet know what I would be.

Three months later I finished all the first semester courses and returned to school since I had got much better. The teachers praised me for my hard study and asked other students to learn from me. However, at that time a student who did well in studies was not considered useful. In discussing my application to be a member of the Chinese Communist Youth League, Lao Qin said, 'Her study is good enough and her qualities are fine but her health is not good. I still think she needs more physical labour. Otherwise she can't be a successor of our revolution.'

I wasn't given permission to join the Youth League until Lao Qin left the school a few months later. I don't know where he went and I never heard of him again.

A wonderful thing happened during our years in the countryside. In August 1971, when I was fourteen, my mother gave birth to another daughter, whom she named Hui. Even though it had been such a long time since there'd been a baby in the house, my parents were delighted and there was no question that she added to the happiness of our family. I doted on my new sister, who, like me, was a long baby, and helped look after her when I got back from school. Needless to say, my grandmother had once again been distraught at the addition of yet another girl to the family, but in spite of this, as the years went by, the two of them grew to love each other greatly.

待业青年

JOB-WAITING YOUTH

By the early 1970s the Chinese economy was in a very bad state as a result of the Cultural Revolution. All through that turmoil, the premier, Zhou Enlai, had kept his position because he was so highly regarded throughout the country. But in 1972 Zhou got cancer, and Mao Zedong was also in poor health. Zhou, who could see that something had to be done to lift economic production, convinced Mao that he needed a capable assistant and succeeded in having Deng Xiaoping reinstated as vice-premier. Deng had a good economic mind and had earlier been accused of being a capitalist-roader; he was removed from his post and sent to the countryside in Jiangxi. With his return to power in early 1973, many other high-ranking cadres were also allowed to resume their old positions.

In that same year my family was allowed to return to Nanchang. My father took up his old job in the Nanchang People's Bank while my mother worked in the Association of Science and Technology. Jing and I went to the Nanchang Number 6 High School. A classmate told me that in the last few years of the Cultural Revolution, due to the prevailing opinion of 'study is useless' which had exerted a tremendous influence in city schools, students had acquired little cultural knowledge. What they had learnt was mostly political propaganda. After Deng Xiaoping became vice-premier, schools started to stress study again and to criticise the idea that study is useless. After my first tests in all subjects, I found I had learnt much more in my previous school than my new classmates had in theirs. I got excellent results in every subject, and especially in Chinese and English. Before long I was elected to be monitor and Youth League branch secretary of my class.

In the summer of 1974 I was seventeen and was to graduate from high school. Although universities had resumed enrolment after being closed during the Cultural Revolution, their doors were only open to workers, peasants and soldiers. Graduates of high schools still had no chance for further study in universities, but had to go to the countryside to receive peasants' re-education, the only road before us. This Party policy had been in place since 1968, but there were two exceptions whereby students could stay in the cities: those who were the only children of their family, and those who had serious diseases which prevented them from carrying out physical labour. Cases of the latter had to be confirmed by the relevant department, and such students amounted to less than 2 per cent. Of course, there were also fortune's favourites – non-workers and non-peasants who joined the army 'through the back door' (by improper, even illegal, means). During the 1970s in China, being a soldier was considered the best outlet for young people. They were called *chu lu bing*, which means someone with prospects.

I was not the only child of my family. While my health wasn't strong, I didn't have a serious disease, and my parents didn't want to break with their principles and go through the back door, though the director of the Municipal Committee of Conscription was my father's old friend. They thought it was not respectable and was unfair to others. So I faced leaving my family to become a new peasant.

It was while I was preparing to go to the countryside that the government announced a new policy whereby a family was allowed to keep one child in a city, no matter how many children it had. Ping was working in a factory in Xinjian county, so Jing would avoid leaving home after I had left. On hearing this news, my grandmother, who was worried about my future, called my parents to her bed and urged them, 'Ling is not strong enough to do physical labour. I don't care how you do it, but what I request is that you keep her with you. Otherwise I won't be at peace when I die.'

Concerned at grandmother's words, my parents, after deep thought, decided that I should stay in Nanchang instead of Jing. This decision made me feel very guilty when, two years later, as soon as she graduated from high school, Jing was sent to be re-educated two hundred kilometres away.

I also felt a more immediate shame before my classmates, most of whom were going to the countryside. It was customary before leaving to make a public speech expressing enthusiasm about following Chairman Mao's directives and learning from the peasants. As a student cadre – I was vice-president of the students' union – I should have been one of those making such a speech, but because of my parents' decision I could not. I felt like an army deserter sneaking away on the eve of battle and could not bear to face my classmates. I asked for a long period of sick leave until they had all left. For many years I regretted that I didn't even see them off and say goodbye.

Leaving home and going to the countryside to be a peasant was very hard, but staying home was not easy either. We did nothing but wait to be assigned work in a factory. We got a common name – job-waiting youth. Each year the Bureau of Labour gave quotas for a certain number of jobs to the local residents' committees, which were in charge of assigning them. Anyone wanting a job in China had to be registered with a residents' committee, the director of which was appointed by the government and whose members were retired people and housewives. They decided who should be given a job as it came up on the basis of who was neediest, and because my family was not in financial trouble, I had to wait a long time.

Unlike most of the job-waiting youth, I didn't care when I got a job. What I cared more about was looking after my grandmother and doing my own study. Seven months later, my grandmother died. I had never before experienced such extreme sorrow. I will always remember what she said to me when she died: 'Ling, I'm dying but I have no regrets, except I haven't seen you become a university student. I do believe you will have bright prospects if you only keep studying, and learn as much and widely as you can.' Though my study was aimless, I persevered with reading and writing. I read every book my hands could reach: ancient and modern, Chinese and foreign. I wrote poems, short stories and essays.

Then in the autumn of 1975, one year after I'd left high school, China resumed diplomatic relations with Japan. Japanese was suddenly regarded as an important foreign language and I discovered that the Nanchang Adults Night College was offering enrolment in a course in Japanese. I went along and found out that I was ineligible to enrol. The registrar told me that the college, as with all the universities, only enrolled people who were working. I was asked to provide a letter from my work unit to prove I was employed there. I had set out in high spirits and came back disappointed. Where could I get such a letter? A friend of mine offered me an idea. 'You can ask your father or your mother's work unit to help you,' she said. It sounded good, but I couldn't ask my parents to do that. And I knew they wouldn't do it for me anyway.

On the night the course started, I went to the college and found the classroom. There were about forty lucky people in it, and the top of each desk bore the student's name. There were no spare desks and chairs. The teacher was an old man with a kindly face. He was tall and thin and his hair had turned grey but he looked spirited. He concentrated intently on his teaching and I thought he hadn't noticed me, an unlucky girl standing at the back door of the classroom. I persuaded myself that it was not too bad to stand there attending the course. I had merely bought a standing ticket while the others had bought seats. Also, it was not shameful – I was standing there for nothing but study. I made up my mind to be a 'standing student' as long as the teacher didn't throw me out.

The teacher did not ask me to leave but gave his comments on my assignments, which I handed in along with the other students. One night, after four weeks, I stood against the door as usual and was surprised to hear the teacher calling my name. He pointed to a desk and chair that had been added to the last row and said, 'You can take that seat. It's better than standing.' I could barely believe what I had heard. I was allowed to sit in. I nodded with great appreciation and said to myself, Now I'm a lucky girl too.

In the semester examination my result was among the best in the class, and I became the teacher's favourite pupil. The college made an exception and received me as a formal student, and after the second semester I not only attended the course in Japanese, but also courses in English, Chinese, foreign classical literature, prose and poetry, philosophy, political economy, and Lu Xun's works (Lu Xun was the greatest writer in China in the early days of the twentieth century). I spent almost every night in the college and most of my other time in study.

At the beginning of 1976 I heard the news that the Bureau of Education was recruiting casual teachers of Chinese. I thought I was qualified, as I had been the best in the class in this subject at high school and had further studied it for six months at the college. After an examination and a teaching test I received an acceptance letter. But in the same mail as this correspondence, I received another letter – from the Residents' Committee, which said it was now my turn to get a job. The job I was to be given was an inspector in a shoe factory.

There is a proverb in China: 'Lucky things always come in

pairs, and misfortunes never come singly.' Fate had brought me to the crossroads. Holding the two letters, I couldn't say I was happy or vexed; it was too hard to make a choice between the two jobs. If I chose the first one, I would have more time to study, but it was only a temporary job. If I chose the second, I would have a permanent position and my parents need not worry about my employment any longer – but the cost for this was giving up my study.

My parents encouraged me to make the decision myself. 'A person who faces a choice is both lucky and unlucky,' my father said. 'Usually you lose one thing while you gain another at the same time. This is dialectical logic. What to consider is which is more important to you.'

My mother said, 'No matter which job you choose, we will support you. But you should think it through carefully before you decide, otherwise you will regret it afterwards.'

The next day, I told my decision to my friends. Everyone was shocked and thought I was mad.

'You're really silly to give up such a nice job to take casual work.'

'What is the use? You always study and study, every day. You have already been a bookworm.'

'Everyone wants a permanent job. You shouldn't give it up so easily. Don't be divorced from reality.'

That evening, when my parents came home, I told them my decision and what my friends had said. I thought my mother and father might make the same comments; all parents hope their children will have stable jobs. But to my surprise, they smiled and said, 'We knew what your choice would be. We're pleased you have so much courage. Take your own road, don't mind what others say. We believe you will have a better future than a factory worker.'

I was moved by their words. They gave me courage and confidence. I felt fortunate to have such sympathetic parents and I was very appreciative of their understanding and support. It was this choice which laid the foundation for my later enrolling in university and becoming a judge.

坎坷之路

TWISTS AND TURNS

One year after I became a temporary high-school teacher at Jiang Jun Du school, the central government announced a new policy on university enrolments. Entrance examinations were to be resumed, and anyone under the age of 45 who had graduated from high school had the right to sit the examination. Everyone knew that getting into university didn't only mean having a stable job, but also meant becoming a state cadre, working in an office. (In China at that time, the term 'cadre' was similar to 'white collar' in Western countries.) This new policy meant that a great number of people between the ages of seventeen and forty-four could be examined, but only 2 per cent of them would be the lucky ones. As a lot of work was needed to prepare for the examinations, the autumn term of 1977 was delayed until the spring of 1978.

I was delighted to have the chance to enrol at university. I planned to major in law, a course which at that time was offered by only a few universities. All my life I had admired my father and when I was sixteen I learnt that he had been a judge in the army, something which had a great influence on me. I dreamt of one day becoming a judge just like him. And the older I grew, the more I understood the importance of law to a society. China needed the law and it needed people to execute it.

I got an application form which asked for my intended major and my preferred university. I told my parents my plans at dinner, but they didn't make any comment until I was going to bed.

'Ling,' my mother said, coming to sit on the edge of my bed, 'I should respect your decision as usual, but there is one thing I want to say as it worries me so much. You know your father used to be a military judge –'

'That's why I chose law,' I interrupted. 'I want to be a judge too.'

My mother looked solemn. 'Well, it's a great ideal, but that's exactly why I'm scared. You're too young to understand how difficult it is to be judge. It's too close to politics. You've been a good daughter – accept my advice now and choose any subject but law.'

Seeing my mother's serious expression, I didn't argue any more, although I was still not very clear about what had happened to my father. My sisters and I had asked him many times about his troubled past, but he always kept silent on his personal details and told us instead about the battles he'd been in and the cases he'd tried. If we pushed too hard my mother would interrupt: 'Don't ask these unhappy questions. You're too young to understand.'

Reluctantly I gave up my ideal and applied instead to study Japanese language at the Shanghai Foreign Languages

Institute, a prestigious institution. Besides Japanese, I had to take five other academic tests – politics, Chinese, history, geography and mathematics. To be successful, I had to pass both the language test and the other subjects.

Two weeks later, I got the results. My total marks for the five subjects were above the pass line and in my Japanese test I came first out of more than a hundred applicants. I was very excited, particularly when my friends and relatives congratulated me. I knew that the institute would accept only two students from Nanchang for the Japanese course, but since I'd got the highest mark I was sure I'd be one of them.

I hurried to tell my mother as soon as she came home. I was sure she'd be very pleased at the news.

'I knew it would be like this. I'm really proud of you. But . . . ' Her smile disappeared.

'What do you mean?'

'Now, one thing has been worrying me – the political examination. You know your father's and my work units must issue proof of our political histories. It will affect you if your father's unit provides a copy of his personal file.'

My heart suddenly sank. At that time, everyone who was working had a personal file. This was actually a political file which recorded important events such as joining the Party, being awarded a prize or being given a punishment. It would follow the person everywhere and influence the rest of their life. Once a person got a bad record in their file, they would have little chance of getting a good job elsewhere or being promoted. Furthermore, the file would also influence their children's future.

I knew my father's file would record the medals he had been awarded during the war, but it would also have details of the punishments he'd received during the Anti-Rightist Campaign and the Cultural Revolution. There was a possibility I might not pass the political examination, and to some extent this would be more influential than my academic results. I was reminded of the brother of a classmate of mine, a talented young man who loved the army, having served in it since he was fourteen. After eight years he was forced to leave because of his father's political problems, and soon after he took his own life.

That night I hardly slept. I imagined various results. I hoped the person who was going to issue the letter would be kind. The next day I anxiously awaited my father's return home. I can still remember how nervous we were when he showed us a yellow sealed envelope. It was thin – it could be only one piece of paper. My father didn't know its content as he was not allowed to see it or ask about it; that was the discipline. He gave it to me and told me to send it to the Municipal Advanced Education Recruitment Office.

I held the envelope up close to the light and to my surprise I could see some words. I strained to read them. ' . . . had no important political problem . . . ' I cheered up. 'I've passed, I've passed.' My parents took a long breath.

After I'd sent off the letter I went to the cemetery and told my grandmother the good news. I wanted to set her mind at ease.

One week passed, then another week, and I received nothing. I waited, waited and waited anxiously, while many others enjoyed their good news. When the recruitment period was almost finished, I still hadn't received either an admission or a failure notice, but news finally came from a friend of my mother's. I was told that two applicants had already been notified of their admission to the Shanghai Foreign Languages Institute. This made me extremely disappointed – I could not accept this cruel fact. It seemed that I had been thrown down into a bottomless chasm. I locked myself in my room and refused to eat anything or see anybody all day.

'You are unlucky. It must be that someone took up your seat through the back door,' a friend of mine said from outside my room.

'Don't be too sad. You're still young. Try again next time,' a relative tried to comfort me.

'Be strong! You've just begun your lifelong journey and you may meet many more difficulties or failures. If you fall down at this reversal, how will you handle them later?' advised my father.

'I hope my daughter can withstand any setbacks,' said my mother.

At night I lay in bed thinking repeatedly of my parents' words. They were right. How could I be beaten down so easily? What did I look like? A coward, a craven? I regretted my behaviour.

The next morning I bestirred myself and made a promise to my parents: 'Don't worry about me any more. I will face any wind and waves bravely.' Then I went straight away to the Provincial Advanced Education Recruitment Office. I wanted to find out what had happened.

A young man who looked very polite received me. I showed him the report of my examination marks and asked him to explain why I hadn't received any notice.

'I'll check for you. Please take a seat.' I followed him into the office and sat in a chair.

He took out a thick file from a cabinet against the wall and turned it page by page. I thought he might be looking for my name. After a few minutes, he put the file back and handed my examination report to an old man sitting near the window. They talked in low voices for a while.

'I'm sorry.' The young man came to me. 'Your marks are very high and should be on the list sent by the Municipal Recruitment Office. Unfortunately I can't find your name, that's why you haven't been recruited. I think your file must be still in the municipal office. You'd better contact them.'

I left and walked the distance to the municipal office. It was very quiet; only one woman was inside. She didn't let me finish my words and said rudely, 'Our work has finished. If you got good marks, you must have passed the primary selection and your file must have been sent to the provincial office.'

'Are you sure you've sent my file to the provincial office? I just came from there. They said they haven't had it.'

'Impossible. Go ask them again.' She waved her hand dismissively.

The responses from the two offices left me confused. I knew one was wrong but I couldn't judge which that was. I didn't want to give up and I decided to get to the bottom of things, no matter how they kicked me back and forth like a ball.

There were more than three kilometres between the two offices. I felt my legs getting heavier. It was lunchtime when I got back to the provincial office and I had to wait outside. One hour later, I met the young man again. He was angry at the answer I had been given by the woman at the municipal office.

He made a phone call. 'We definitely haven't received this applicant's file. You'd better check it once again.' He turned to me. 'She's checking. We will know the result soon.'

We didn't get a phone call from the woman until four-forty, twenty minutes before knocking-off time.

'Yes, it's here,' she told the man. 'We made a mistake and put her file together with those of the failed applicants. It was done by accident. You know, there were too many files. We apologise for this.'

'Why didn't they send me a failure notice then, since they put my file away with the failed ones?' I asked the young man. 'Can you check for me who has been recruited?'

He hesitated for a while and then went to another office, coming back with a sheet of paper in his hand. I learnt that the applicants who had been recruited had not attended the test for Japanese, but English. The reason given for their recruitment was that no applicant who had attended the Japanese test had reached the pass line.

Later, I understood the real reason was that both of them were *guanxi hu* (had a close relationship with the power-holders). Because of my high marks, the municipal office had to contrive an accident that made my file disappear. I didn't know to whom I should complain, or even where I could lodge a complaint. I only knew that all my efforts for realising my dream had been wasted.

'Sorry,' the young man said gently.

Sorry? Could that make up for what I had lost? I wondered if the cadres had thought of my mood, the mood of a girl who had been yearning to study and dreaming of getting into university.

After the traditional Spring Festival in February 1978, when many young people were going to university, I started to prepare my teaching plan for the new term. One morning, a colleague gave me a letter from the Provincial Advanced Education Recruitment Office. I opened it, puzzled. Inside was an admission notice – it said that the English Department of the Branch College of Jiangxi Normal Institute had recruited me.

I knew this branch college, it was newly established and was a lower level than university – similar to Australian TAFE colleges. Branch colleges selected their students later than universities did, since they often took students who failed to gain entry to the latter. Should I accept or not? Again I faced a hard choice. If I had registered for the examination for an English major, I would have gained entry to a better university than a branch college.

My colleagues in the office crowded me, all talking at once. I didn't know who to listen to.

'Don't be hesitant. Anyway, it's better than being a temporary teacher.'

'If you're sure you can do well in the exam next year and

be accepted into a better university, then you can give up your place in the branch college. But if you're not sure, and you sit the exam next year and do badly, then you'll have nothing.'

'I don't agree with you. Of course she'll be successful next year.'

When I showed the letter to my parents, they let me make my own decision as usual. I thought about the matter again and again, and made a final decision about three weeks later.

By then the term was already two weeks old. I put some books and clothes in a suitcase and went to the college by myself. It was far from the city and it took me almost an hour to get there by bus. I found my way to the administration office, where I met the director. As soon as I introduced myself, everyone in the office stared at me.

'Aha! It's you, Wang Ling.' The director looked me up and down. 'How proud you are! You don't want to enter our college, do you? You look down on our college. Why do you come today?'

I hadn't expected the college to receive me this way. The director's impolite manner, sharp words, and other people's unfriendly expressions made me uncomfortable. I knew this was a bad beginning and tried to change my situation by explaining.

'I'm sorry for being late. Indeed, I have been hesitating to accept your offer. It's because I'm afraid my English is not good enough.' I thought this might be the best excuse.

'Don't lie to me. I know your English is better than many other students we have recruited,' said the director. 'Since you have come, we welcome you. But you must submit a written *jian tao* (self-criticism) as you are late. Otherwise . . .'

I couldn't believe my ears. Write a self-criticism? That was the hallmark of bad students. I had been a good student since I first entered primary school.

'I have never written a self-criticism before and I won't write one now – or later.' I couldn't control myself.

'No problem. We should reconsider your entrance then.'

'You needn't. I give it up now.' I was shivering with anger. 'Please return my personal file to the recruitment office.'

'Well, that's our business. Maybe, if we would like . . .'

From the director's laughter, I knew I had made a big mistake that could damage my future. If they didn't send my file back, I would still be their student on the form. That meant I would have no right to attend the examinations next year. I either had to get my file back or hand in a written self-criticism. My self-respect made me choose the former.

I left the college and went directly to the Provincial Recruitment Office. After hearing my report, the director looked at me strangely.

'You are too young and too serious,' he said. 'What will it hurt you to write a self-criticism? I wrote dozens of them during the Cultural Revolution. How can I help you now? I think you'd better go back to the college and express your apology.'

'Impossible. You know it was your dereliction of duty that caused today's situation. What I need you to do is confirm that I have the right to attend the examinations next year.'

'I've never done that before and I'm afraid I can't now. I'll give you a suggestion. Go talk with the education minister for Jiangxi province. He is also the director of the Advanced

Education Recruitment Committee. Everything will be all right as long as he says yes.'

The committee was a higher level than the office, and was in charge of both the municipal and provincial recruitment offices. When I got there, a few people were waiting outside.

'Is this the minister's office?' I asked a man.

'Yes, but he won't see anyone as he is in a meeting. We've waited for nearly two hours.'

I couldn't wait, I was burning with impatience. I stepped forward and knocked on the door. It opened. The room was full of people and smoke, and everyone looked at me when I put my head in. As soon as I said who I was looking for, all eyes turned to an old man sitting at a big desk near the window.

'I'm sorry to interrupt you,' I said to the old man, 'but I have an urgent problem. Can you give me one minute?'

Unexpectedly, the old man stood up and walked out. A tall, big man with grey hair, he looked like a military commander but his expression was amiable. He listened patiently to my story and appeared disappointed by his staff's mistake. After I submitted my request, he kept quiet.

'It's only permission but to me it's a chance, a hope. Only you can help me now,' I implored in a voice choked with sobs.

'Don't be upset. Of course I will help you. It's our fault.' He thought for a while. 'I'll ring the Provincial Recruitment Office and ask them to give you a confirmation letter. You need to go there to pick it up, and then go back home and make good preparation for the exams next time.'

I should have been studying in a classroom at the

Shanghai Foreign Languages Institute, but instead all I had after having made great efforts was a chance, only a chance, of applying to sit the entrance exams again. Holding the confirmation letter, I didn't know whether to laugh or cry.

Everything returned to normal. I went to my school as usual as a temporary teacher. The only difference was that I was now asked to teach English as well as Chinese. The principal said it was a pity he hadn't known I understood English as teachers were badly needed. He didn't care how much English knowledge I had and assigned me to teach two classes, at grades seven and eight. My workload increased a lot but I was pleased because I regarded working as a kind of study, and the more I worked, the more I would study.

Although I felt very tired when I got back home every day, I still had to study at nights. The examinations for 1978 were to be held in July, only five months away, but I still hadn't made up my mind which major to choose. I was afraid the same thing would happen if I persisted in Japanese. Maybe I'd better choose English – the competition was strong but there was a much higher quota than for Japanese.

I made a final decision after a chance meeting with an old man. I was attending a series of seminars for English teachers on Saturday mornings where the invited guest was Lao Cai, whose face was glowing with health though he was near seventy. His voice was loud and clear and he spoke English with an American accent. He had been a missionary and had studied and lived in

America for more than twenty years, from the 1920s to the 1940s. In order to express his love for the new China after the Communist Party took over in 1949, he had brought his wife, a piano performer, and their five daughters and one son back to China. He suffered a lot during the Cultural Revolution because of his background and was criticised as an American spy. His house and some valuables were confiscated and his wife's piano was damaged. His four younger children were assigned to different areas in the countryside or outlying districts, and he and his wife were thrown out to live in an attic of an old house. When the Cultural Revolution ended in 1976, his political life was liberated and he became a member of the Standing Committee of the Provincial Political Consultative Committee.

'I'm glad to be here to give you a lecture.' Lao Cai looked very excited. 'I would like to do something for our country, though I am already old.'

Throughout his classes he patiently helped us with grammar and pronunciation; he brought us interesting articles and short stories to read, and asked us relevant questions. I always displayed my knowledge actively. On the last morning, when the lecture was over, Lao Cai came up to me and smiled. 'You have a good basis of English. Why haven't you entered university?' he asked.

I told him that my Japanese was actually better than my English, and gave him my unlucky story. He sympathised and made me a generous offer.

'I am happy to help you with your English if you'd like to apply for entrance to the subject,' he said.

This unexpected luck decided me. I didn't hesitate any longer but settled on English as a major.

Lao Cai made a study plan for me. I worked in the daytime and went to see him on Tuesday, Thursday and Saturday evenings, for two hours each time. I was warmly welcomed by Lao Cai and his wife from the start, and when we began our first lesson I understood that he had prepared lessons just for me. I was moved and vowed I would prove myself worthy of his kindness by gaining good marks in the exam.

He gave me a test of three pages, and after I'd completed it he checked it carefully and marked the errors. He didn't mind explaining things again and again until I mastered them completely. He lectured me on the relevant grammar, and before I left he arranged some extensive reading for my homework.

A few months later, I got the examination application form. In the column for subject and university choice, I confidently filled in 'English major, Anhui University'. I had two reasons for choosing this university. One was that the English department had some outstanding teachers, equal in quality to those of the famous foreign languages institutes in Shanghai and Beijing, and the other was that Anhui province was one of the poorer provinces at that time. The university was in the capital, Hefei, to the north of Jiangxi. Since Hefei was a small city and its living conditions not as good as other, larger cities, I thought that people who needed to enter university through the back door might not choose to go there. I hoped to avoid being elbowed out again.

Shortly before the examinations, my nervousness, the

amount of work I was doing, and the pressure I felt to be on me all took their toll and I fell ill. My temperature rose to 39° and my blood pressure dropped to 85/55. Seeing my thin, tired faced, my mother grew worried.

'You look so weak, how can you sit for the examinations?'

In order to lessen my mother's anxiety, on the morning of the first examination I pretended to feel better. Actually, I had a bad headache and my legs were shaking when I walked into the hall. My father, like the parents of many students taking the examinations, had asked for those days off work, and he went with me to the hall each time, waiting outside until I'd finished. Politics, Chinese, mathematics, history, geography and English – at last, three days and six subjects were completed. I relaxed and lay in bed for three days.

I didn't disappoint my parents and Lao Cai, getting excellent results in every subject, and in September 1978 I was fortunate enough to be accepted into Anhui University. As the saying goes, the road to happiness is strewn with setbacks. After many twists and turns, I had at last taken the first step toward my career.

坎坷之路

FATHER

One month later, I caught the train to Shanghai, where I was to transfer to another for Hefei. It was the first time I had left home alone. My parents, sisters and friends accompanied me to Nanchang station. Once on board I looked at my parents standing on the platform, their faces old and worn, and all sorts of feelings welled up in me. I had thousands of things I wanted to say but failed to utter a single one. I only swore in my heart, Dear Father and Mother, I will value this opportunity and make good use of my time to study assiduously. One day I will repay you for your loving kindness with my achievements.

The platform was crowded with people who'd come to see off their children, relatives or friends. When the train started moving slowly, the platform echoed with goodbyes. I choked back my tears and waved to my family and friends. 'Take care! Bye! I will write to you.' My mother couldn't help shedding tears. She waved her hand as she ran, following the train, waving and running till the train left the station.

Twenty-five hours later, I got off at Hefei station, along with many other new students. The university bus collected us and drove us to the campus. Looking at the words 'Anhui University' on the gate and the slogans 'Welcome new students' on the walls, I felt my heart beating fast, excited that I had at last become a university student.

Members of the students' union helped us carry our luggage to the dormitory, a three-storey building in a small yard. My room was on the third floor and I was to share it with five other new students from different provinces. The room was not big: four double bunks on each side, a table against the window and, by the door, two wall cabinets. We'd all brought at least one big suitcase and a few boxes, and the only place for these was the spare bunk by the door. We stacked them up with the heavier things on the bottom and the lighter ones on top.

At midday we were taken to the dining hall. Meals were being sold from eight windows and dozens of students were lined up before every one. A blackboard menu hung on the wall beside each window and in a corner of the hall was another window selling meal tickets. We had to go and buy the meal tickets first and then use them to pay for the dishes we chose. The food was very plain, with a choice of only three dishes, all of which were served out of enormous basins. They were nothing like the delicious meals my mother cooked, and I found myself longing for my favourites – sweet and sour spareribs, stir-fried shredded pork with green pepper, stir-fried beef with radish, diced chicken with cucumber and a sweet sauce made from soy beans and flour, and duck braised in soy sauce. Here every student had their own bowl, which had to do for rice as well as any other dishes, and after we'd eaten we had to wash them ourselves. Just outside the dining hall was a long row of taps for this purpose.

After lunch, the vice-director of the English department showed us around the campus – the lecture rooms, library, meeting hall, sports centre and grounds. We were issued with student identity cards, university badges, library cards and medical cards, as well as English books and earphones. We were also given the use of one wooden stool each for our time at the university. There were no chairs or other seats in our dormitories and we had to sign for a stool and be personally responsible for it.

On my first night in the dormitory I barely slept. I was too excited and couldn't stop thinking, and I was also afraid of the mice. In the moonlight I saw that there were six or seven large rodents running around on the floor, making an annoying noise. I had never seen such a thing before and was so scared I wrapped my quilt closely around myself as I stared at them. Suddenly a scream made me sit bolt upright. Everyone was woken up. The light was turned on and Li Ping, whose bed was opposite mine, jumped out of her bed, shaking all over and shouting, 'Something bit my toe!'

'It was a mouse,' I said quickly.

'A mouse?' The whole dormitory gazed at me in surprise. 'How do you know?'

I told them I had seen several mice, which made everyone scared, and we kept the light on. Even so, I couldn't sleep. I kept imagining I could feel a mouse climbing up to my bed, about to bite my toe, and this fear swept my excited thoughts clean away. The next morning my eyes were bloodshot and I felt homesick for the first time since I'd left. I even regretted having chosen this university and thought of leaving.

My low mood lasted for two weeks, until the general office of the university took action to wipe out the mice. Before long I grew accustomed to the not-so-good living conditions and concentrated on my study. We had six subjects in the first term – the history of the Communist Party of China, Chinese composition, English listening, intensive reading, extensive reading, and physical education. Along with my classmates I did not like studying the history of the CPC, which we had once a week. It wasn't that we didn't enjoy learning about it, but we got confused by it constantly changing. One week the teacher would be lecturing us about a historical figure being a capitalist-roader, and the next, because the central government had announced that person's rehabilitation, the teacher would have to begin by explaining that they hadn't actually been a reactionary after all. We couldn't keep up.

Although I lost all interest in the history course, I still had to attend it and take notes and be able to answer the teacher's questions during class. One day, I heard my name called and stood up quickly to answer the question, and another student, a male, did the same thing. We looked at each other, then both sat down, causing an outburst of laughter.

'Who did you call? Wang Ling or Wang Lin?' one student asked.

'Wang Lin.' The teacher pointed to me.

'She is Wang Ling. He is Wang Lin.'

'Oh, she is Wang Lin and he is also Wang Lin.' The

teacher was from southern China and could not pronounce 'Ling' clearly. In order to avoid confusion, he never called either of us again. That was good for me, I didn't need to worry about the questions he asked. After that, I brought an English book to read in his class.

The content of the English classes was very simple, almost elementary, with the teacher asking us to spend time practising pronunciation before a mirror. So the course I enjoyed most was Chinese composition, where we not only practised writing but also studied literary theory and works of excellence. Our first assignment was a piece of prose on an open theme. Mine was titled 'Hardly Faded from My Memory', and was about my childhood during the Cultural Revolution. It got a high mark. The teacher read it aloud in both the Chinese and English departments, and it was later published in the university newspaper. I had a serious talk with my teacher Li about this.

'You did a very good job,' he said. 'Why didn't you choose a major of Chinese literature? You could become a good writer, I believe.'

I told him I had been keen on writing since I was a little girl, and that maybe I would be a good writer in the future, once I'd retired, but not now. I felt confident in my writing.

'What would you like to be after graduation? Interpreter, translator?'

'Neither. What I really want to be is a judge.'

'A judge?' Li was surprised. 'You want to be a judge?'

'Yes. I want to be an upright judge. That's my ideal.'

'Your ideal is beautiful, but it is unrealistic. How can you be a just judge in a society which has no proper legal system, not even strict regulations?'

'I have no idea yet. But I still want to be one.' I wasn't willing to give up my dream, even though I recognised the difficulties ahead.

'It would be a pity to waste your literary talent.' Li shook his head.

I joked that I would give full play to it once I had retired, after a rich life and much work experience.

But I was disturbed by Li's question as to how I could be a just judge in the present-day China without a proper legal system. Since 1949 the central government had laid down over a hundred regulations and rules but most of them had been ignored, especially during the wild days of the Cultural Revolution. I couldn't forget an event which had happened in 1971 in a village close to the one we were living in, near Liantang.

The head of the village had a disabled son. When this son was five years old, the man adopted a two-year-old girl to be his future daughter-in-law. He got a marriage certificate from the relevant office and arranged the wedding for them when the girl was sixteen. The girl refused to get married and ran away from home. A week later she was found and taken back. The head declared to the people of the village who were looking on, 'This girl should be punished because she has broken my family rule and the rule of our village.' In traditional China, the command of parents and the good offices of a matchmaker were considered to be the law in contracting a marriage. The head ordered two of his relatives to tie his adopted daughter up and beat her black and blue.

'Now is the new China!' someone shouted from the crowd. 'You're breaking the state law.'

'What's the state law?' the head demanded. 'My words are the state law.'

No other response came. The people watched as the two men pulled the girl into a dark room, where the head had the men assist his disabled son to violate her. A few days later, news spread that the girl had killed herself by cutting her wrist. The village head denied that his son had raped the girl and used the lame excuse that his son was her lawful future husband. He told the people that as the girl had taken her own life, by herself, nobody was responsible, and he warned that anyone who was meddlesome would pay for it.

The village choked with silent fury. Time passed, and eventually no one talked about the matter any more. In fact, the girl was only one of many victims. China at that time was ruled by men. The legal system was almost at a standstill: power was stronger than the law, and people who held power could get away with anything. The legal organs were nothing more than the tools of the power-holders. Thinking back on this incident, I felt I had slim hopes of realising my ideal of a fair legal system.

In the late winter of 1978 the ground was covered by thick snow and no one expected an early spring. But a great change took place in China that year when the central government declared that the Party's main task would now be to modernise and strengthen the socialist legal system. As part of the drive toward this, a series of basic codes was enacted.

On 1 July 1979 the Criminal Law of the People's Republic of China and the Criminal Procedure Law of the People's Republic of China were adopted by the Fifth National People's Congress. Both came into effect on 1 January 1980 and were followed by many others, covering marriage, ethnic minorities in China, the rights of people who were arrested and detained, business practices, capital loans and joint ventures. These laws marked a departure from the chaotic years of the Cultural Revolution. At the start of that movement, not even Liu Shaoqi, the Vice-Chairman of the People's Republic of China, had the protection of the law. In 1967 a huge rally in Tiananmen Square, attended by over a hundred thousand people, denounced Liu as the number one public enemy, and even though Liu called on the rights guaranteed him in the constitution, he was denied a trial and sent to prison, where he later died.

In contrast, Jiang Qing and her Gang of Four were given completely different legal treatment. Their trial in 1980 marked the first time lawyers were seen back in courts since the Cultural Revolution, and the case was tried in accordance with the new criminal law. Jiang Qing had been an actress before marrying Mao Zedong and prior to the Cultural Revolution had no formal position in the Party or government. But during the Cultural Revolution she came to assume enormous power, still without holding any formal position, and along with the other three members of her gang she exercised huge abuses of that power. Because the trial was a major one, whose outcome affected the entire country, the Supreme Court of China set up a special panel consisting of seven senior judges to handle it. All four defendants had their own lawyers, and at the end of the trial all four were found guilty of crimes of counter-revolution and given the death sentence, which was suspended to life imprisonment.

This change in the political situation in the winter of 1978 inspired me with hope. It reminded me of a poem: 'Where the hills and streams end and there seems no road beyond,/Amidst shading willows and blooming flowers another village appears.' I now knew my dream would come true, even though I didn't yet know where the road to being a judge was and I still didn't have the permission of my parents. Nonetheless, I started to collect articles on legal matters from various newspapers and magazines, reference material to prove that China now attached importance to justice and had started to handle legal cases in accordance with the law. I felt I could now answer Teacher Li confidently – I would be able to be an upright, ethical judge in this changed political situation. And I planned to use these changes to convince my parents that their worries were unnecessary.

One evening during the summer holiday of 1980, I took out the material I had collected and showed my parents, piece by piece. They read them carefully, including those they already knew.

'A huge change has occurred in the legal field, hasn't it?' I opened my argument.

'Yes, indeed. The central government has finally realised

the importance of the legal system to a country.' My father appeared to be deeply touched.

But my mother was not optimistic about the future. 'There is a long way to go to become a country ruled by law. If only the changes could go on without wavering.'

'I think the situation will get better and better,' I tried to convince her. 'I know there will be over a hundred new regulations and rules coming into force in the next few years. The courts are handling cases independently now, free of political interference from any individual or organisation.'

'You still really want to be a judge, don't you?' Mother understood me well.

'Yes, I have never given up,' I admitted.

'But you *must* give up,' my mother said with a determined attitude.

I looked at my father for help. He kept silent, with a gloomy expression on his face. I didn't know why my parents, who'd always respected their children's opinions and choices, were so opposed to me on this matter. I thought it must be related to my father's experiences as a judge, which he never talked about with us. He had often told us stories about the battles he had participated in in the army, giving detailed explanations and vivid descriptions of the War of Liberation, but my sisters and I knew nothing about his time as a judge.

I took a deep breath. 'Father, I have been wanting to ask you a question for a long time but I am scared.'

'Go on, please.'

'Tell me something about your past, your experiences as a

military judge. It may help me to understand why Mother and you are so against me being one.'

My father heaved a sigh and patted me gently on the head. 'It was nearly thirty years ago. I don't even want to think of it. But since you are unshakeable in your determination, I think I'd better tell you. You must promise me, though, to reconsider your aspiration afterwards.'

'Yes, I promise.' Seeing his serious expression, I nodded repeatedly, and for the first time I heard the complete story of my father's life.

He was born in 1930 in the town of Ping Gang in Xifeng county of Liaoning province, near the border of what is now North Korea. His father was a fur dealer who led a well-to-do life. My father had a brother and a sister and was the youngest of the three. He studied for six years at primary school and three years at high school, and was consistently the cleverest and naughtiest student in his class. He often received prizes for his good achievements, but he also received regular punishment for his disobedient behaviour. At that time, there was great dignity in the teaching profession. Students respected their teachers as they respected their parents. Teachers' words were taken as imperial edicts and they had the right to punish students by beating their palms with a short plank. Students were asked to extend their hands to the teacher, and after the beating were expected to say thanks. My father couldn't remember how many times he had extended his hand to the teacher during primary school, but one day, shortly before he was to graduate to high school, he refused to comply.

'How dare you disobey my order?' The teacher was annoyed.

'I did nothing wrong this time,' my father argued. 'I pushed him because he bullied that disabled boy.'

'I don't care what reason you have. You must be punished for pushing others down.' The teacher would not listen to my father's explanation but pulled up his left hand. 'You must take five more slaps for contradicting me.'

The teacher finally stopped after fifteen slaps. During his punishment my father stared at the plank, gritting his teeth and resolving to hold out. His palm swelled immediately. He did not say thanks. As a result of this, the teacher sent a girl in the class to fetch his parents. His father was not at home, so his mother hurried to the school alone. When she saw her son's swollen palm, she felt as if a knife had pierced her heart.

'I'm sorry I haven't educated my son well. Please calm your anger.' My grandma had to show her faith in the teacher. She asked my father to apologise.

But instead of an apology, my father shouted at the teacher, 'I shall never be your student. You're not qualified to be my teacher as you don't distinguish clearly between right and wrong.' He ran away from the school and never went back again, enrolling in high school soon afterwards.

Shortly after he left high school, my father joined Lin Biao's liberation army. Lin Biao was the famous commander of the Communist Party's troops, who were seeking to destroy the Nationalist Party – the Guomindang – and with it the whole feudal system of old China. Whenever the Communist Party liberated an area by overthrowing the local tyrants, it would carry out land reform in order to gain the support of the peasants. This civil war had been going on since the 1920s, but it came to a temporary halt in 1937 when the Japanese invaded northern China. From 1937 to 1945 the Communist Party and the Guomindang joined forces to fight a war of resistance against the Japanese, but as soon as Japan was defeated by the allies in World War II, the old struggle was resumed. In August 1945 both Communist and Guomindang troops were sent to northeast China to try and gain control over the three provinces of Liaoning, Jilin and Heilongjiang.

By the end of 1946 Lin Biao's troops had liberated my father's hometown of Ping Gang and established a garrison there. Working to ensure the support of the people, the army set up branches of the Communist Party, the Peasants' Committee and the People's Militia. My father was selected to be the captain of the People's Militia and his older brother was made chairman of the Peasants' Committee, where they worked actively for the communist cause from morning till night.

Meanwhile great battles were still taking place between the communists and the Guomindang in other districts and many young people were volunteering to join the People's Liberation Army. My father was one of them, and early in 1947 he signed on to fight the War of Liberation. He knew my grandma would not approve, so he kept his news secret until the night before he was due to leave.

Then he broke the news. 'I have joined the army and will

leave tomorrow morning. I will come back after the whole country is liberated. My brother and sister will look after you for –'

Without letting my father finish, my grandma burst out crying. 'Our hometown has been liberated already. You have things to do here! Why do you want to leave your home to fight battles? It's very dangerous. You're only sixteen.'

'I have grown up. I am a strong young man now. Don't worry about me.'

'No! I can't let you go.'

'Who will go if every young man must stay at home like me? Our hometown has been liberated but more than half the country hasn't. The people are still living in an abyss of misery. I have a responsibility to help them.' My father tried to convince his mother with the words he'd learnt from the official rhetoric of the army.

'Our son is right. Don't stop him,' my grandfather said.

But my grandma could not stop sobbing.

At five o'clock the next morning, my father got up quietly and tried to leave without alarming his mother, but he was unable to open the door of his room. It was locked; he knew who had done it. He looked around the room to the small window on the back wall, which was higher than he was. He climbed up and peered through it. There was a ditch about a metre away from the house. He would fall into the water unless he jumped vertically, close to the wall, but he had no other choice. He jumped down carefully, missing the ditch, and ran quickly to catch up with the army. He later found out that my grandma cried all day long when she found her beloved son had gone. Before long her eyesight deteriorated; she finally became blind and never saw her son again. Apart from crying, what she did every day was pray for her son's safe return.

My father knew nothing about what had happened to his mother. He had enthusiastically thrown himself into the revolution. Liberating the whole of China and performing meritorious deeds for the people were his lofty ideals. The goal of the War of Liberation was the overthrow of the Guomindang and the establishment of a new China where the vast masses of workers and peasants would be masters of their own country and be free to live happy and plentiful lives. But the war itself was cruel, with casualties of more than ten million on the two sides.

There were three decisive campaigns during the war, the Liaoxi–Shenyang campaign, the Beijing–Tianjin campaign, and the Huaihai campaign. As a soldier of the Fourth Army under the leadership of Lin Biao, my father took part in the Liaoxi–Shenyang campaign, and later, as a captain in the Guards Regiment, he took part in the Beijing–Tianjin campaign. His regiment crossed the Huanghe and the Yangtze rivers, moving south down to Hainan Island, fighting all the way and liberating one place after another. During these battles my father repeatedly distinguished himself in action. He was wounded in the waist and arm, was awarded a first-class medal, two second-class medals and two third-class medals, and was promoted quickly because of his achievements.

In April of 1949 he was assigned to the criminal section of the army's Military Tribunal as a judge. At that time there were few members of the Communist Party who had received much education at all, and my father, who had gone to high school, was comparatively well educated. No qualifications were required for any posts in the People's Liberation Army, including judges. Most of the cases my father dealt with involved soldiers deserting their posts, stealing or damaging property, raping women and getting into fights with one other. He also dealt with cases of corruption. Corporal punishment was prohibited, but the death sentence was retained and applied for severe crimes.

My father well understood how powerful and responsible his work was, so he made a strict principle for himself that he must examine the facts very carefully and distinguish clearly between right and wrong before giving a judgement. He never forgot his experience of being unjustly punished by his teacher and how he had suffered from it, and he was determined not to wrong an innocent.

With his ethical principles, my father's work went smoothly. Ten months later, he was promoted again, and was put in charge of the criminal section. But my father's brilliant future was suddenly destroyed by a frame-up. As the proverb says, 'A storm may arise from a clear sky and bad or good luck befalls men overnight.'

Most of the cases my father heard involved brave soldiers, and some had fine records of service, but they were also human. They too felt *qi qing liu yu* (the seven human emotions: joy, anger, sorrow, fear, love, hate and desire), and sometimes, particularly after fierce fighting, it was easy for them to forget the strict rules that applied to them. My father felt sorry for them.

Soon after the Battle of Hainan in 1951, my father's unit

was ordered back north, and on the way, in Guangdong province, a captain of a scouting force was accused of committing adultery. Because the woman was the concubine of a tyrant, the crime became more serious. Luo, the vice-director of the Military Tribunal, thought the captain had a class problem as he had fallen in love with a woman who was a reactionary. Even though my father had not recommended the death sentence, Luo overruled him and ordered the captain be executed at once.

My father believed that the woman's class status should not affect the judgement handed down to the captain, who had been a good soldier and had served with merit. That should be taken into account, argued my father.

Just at the same time, the post of director of the Military Tribunal was vacant, the previous director having been assigned to army headquarters. Luo desperately wanted the job and believed my father to be his only opponent. He told my father that he would report the adultery case to headquarters, adding that he hoped my father would not indulge in personal spite.

My father knew exactly what he meant. A few months earlier in Hainan, he had heard a case which had caused great offence to Luo. The offender, a rough and peremptory man named Wu, used to be one of Luo's guards and was still his eyes and ears, reporting to him regularly on things he had seen and heard. It was joked that he'd report to Luo if someone passed wind. While even minor mistakes were published in ordinary circumstances, Wu was an exception. Everyone knew that Luo was his supporter, and Luo himself had an influential supporter in army headquarters. The majority of officials and soldiers were frightened of him.

When Luo was appointed vice-director after the liberation of Guangzhou, the capital of Guangdong province, Wu became more and more wanton. He was sent to the Military Tribunal twice, for injuring a soldier and stealing from a local farmer, but both times received only light punishment. The third time, though, was for an unforgivable crime: he shot a fisherman in order to take his fish, an incident that aroused popular indignation. My father tried the case, and in the report he submitted to army headquarters he wrote that there was sufficient evidence to prove that Wu had committed murder. Furthermore, Wu had previously broken military regulations many times and refused to amend his behaviour. In view of this, and in accordance with military law, my father recommended he be sentenced to death. Luo was unable to protect Wu this time, but he had nursed a hatred of my father ever since.

It was just as Luo was ordering the death sentence on the adulterous captain be carried out that the command came from army headquarters to cancel the judgement. This caused Luo to fly into a rage of shame, but my father did not care about Luo's attitude toward him. He continued hearing his cases one by one, not noticing the black clouds quietly gathering over his head.

In June of 1951 the army arrived in Jiujiang, a city in Jiangxi. It had been very hot there. One evening, my father arrived back at his accommodation exhausted after working hard all day. He had been assigned a small room in a one-storey house with only a single bed and a table in it. Too tired to eat dinner or have a wash or even take off his uniform, he fell onto the bed, lying on his back with his pistol beside his pillow. As it was so hot, he left the window open. When he woke up the next morning, the window was still open but the pistol was gone. He was stunned. To a soldier, his gun was as important as his life.

My father jumped up, searching everywhere in that small room for his pistol, again and again. But he failed to find it and had to report the matter to Luo.

'Losing a weapon is a serious mistake, do you understand?' Luo criticised. 'I must report this to headquarters immediately. And you will lose your head if your pistol hurts innocent people.'

Two weeks passed. The pistol hadn't been found and no one had been injured by it. Its disappearance was very strange and my father was dealt with sternly. He was not only given a demerit but was also transferred to civilian work and his Party membership was revoked for one year. In a flash a military judge with a bright future changed to one with dark prospects.

My father was sent to the Number 175 Military Hospital in Jiujiang. A month later, most of the soldiers and officials in his old unit were sent to the war in Korea. Many of them died there. My father was the only survivor among the people in his unit from his hometown.

Three months later, early in 1952, my father was assigned to the Supervisory Committee of the Jiangxi Provincial Industry Bureau. He should have been appointed director, according to the rank he had held in the army, but was made a supervisor because of the demerit he had been given. He accepted the job without complaint, and the first day went to the office to meet the director. He didn't expect this to be a man who had previously been his subordinate in the Military Tribunal. This man told him some astonishing news.

'Just before our unit set out from Jiangxi, a local farmer found your pistol buried under a tree. No doubt it was a frame-up. Many of us suspected Luo did it. We said the disciplinary measures against you should be withdrawn, but Luo objected.' The man advised my father to talk to army headquarters about returning to his former rank.

But my father did not want to appeal to headquarters. He understood what had really happened to him and what the problem was; that even if he were to succeed this time, it did not mean he would succeed next time. He saw how difficult it was to be an upright judge. However, he did not really understand that it was even more difficult to be an upright man. He did not predict that, because of his ethical standards, he would be subjected to persecution again five years later, at the age of twenty-seven, and with his family be made to suffer greatly during the various political movements of the next thirty years.

Hearing my father's story did not shake my resolve. On the contrary, my desire to be a judge was now stronger then ever.

'Please forgive me, Father. I don't need more time to consider. I will never give up my pursuit. I must be a judge, a just judge.' I felt I had a hundred reasons to do so.

'You needn't ask forgiveness. I only hope you'll think about it carefully before making your final decision.'

My mother was very disappointed in me. 'You are crazy! You don't understand the meaning of *qian che zhi jian* (the overturned cart ahead is a warning to the ones behind), do you?'

'I do understand, but these are different times and the situation is different now,' I argued. 'The more upright the judge, the less unjust the judgements.'

'Okay, do what you want, if you don't mind breaking your mother's heart.'

I felt extremely bad at her anguish. She had suffered too much already because of my father. I couldn't cause her further worry about me – I didn't mention the matter again.

At the end of the holidays, I returned to university. I wrote a letter to my parents telling them I would not think further about being a judge but would concentrate on my English course.

I received an answer from my mother very soon, a long letter in which she wrote:

> *After you left home, your father and I discussed your desire once again. Your father is correct. As your parents, we shouldn't interfere in your choice, and moreover, your choice is right. Your ideal is great. We should support you and be proud of you. Please forgive your mother's selfish . . .*

Tears blurred my eyes and I couldn't keep reading.

From that day on I spent more time on my legal study. By then Anhui University had a law department, one of only a few universities in the country to have one. The department was established in 1979, the year after I had started university, and while it still wasn't possible to take a full law degree, courses on law were offered as part of a general degree. As I wasn't enrolled in the law department I just sat in on the classes and did not take the examinations, but I studied as hard as I could. I was determined to repay my parents' faith in me.

一波三折
ENDLESS SETBACKS

Life at university was rich and varied. Besides study, we went to the cinema almost once a week and sometimes had picnics on weekends. We held parties on festival days – New Year's Eve was the busiest day. During the day we cooked and ate in our classrooms and in the evening we attended the party held by the university. Every department provided a few performances.

At the New Year's party of 1981 my class performed a short play in English, directed by our English-literature teacher from America. The play, called *Blue Bike*, related a poor little American boy's misfortune. One day, he found a broken bike on a rubbish heap. It couldn't be ridden but he took it home and showed it to his uncle, with whom he lived. His uncle repaired the bike and painted it blue. The boy was so glad to have a beautiful blue bike that he rode it every day.

One afternoon, his uncle sent him to buy some food. The boy rode his bike to the shop and parked it outside. Unexpectedly, a well-dressed lady stopped him. She looked over the bike, then shouted loudly, 'You have stolen my bike. This is my bike!' Two policemen came to catch the boy. They didn't allow him to explain, just turned to the lady and said very politely, 'You can take the bike back, madam. We'll teach the little skunk.' Then they dragged the boy to his home and reprimanded his uncle. 'Remember that he will be jailed if he steals again.'

What fatuous policemen! What an unfair judgement! I hated the policemen as well as the lady, though I was acting her part.

'America is a country ruled by justice, isn't it?' I asked the American teacher. 'I don't understand how such a thing could have happened there.'

'Making laws is one matter and enforcing them is another. Not everyone who is responsible for executing a law can enforce it fairly.'

'Do you mean that, to some extent, enforcing the law is more important and more difficult than enacting the law?' I was even more aware that the road I had chosen for myself would not be easy, but I thought of the saying, 'Go deep into the mountains, knowing well that there are tigers there.' I would go on, undeterred by any difficulties ahead.

Since I was studying two courses at once, and wasn't even enrolled in one of them, I was always in the library. There I got to know Yuan, the librarian. He told me he admired my spirit and the fact that I studied hard and he gave me special consideration. At that time the library had few books, especially books in foreign languages, and the limited number of copies were in great demand. There were even fewer books relating to law as it was a new subject, and as soon as new texts came in, the law students would borrow them before I even knew about them. A waterside pavilion gets the moonlight first, as the saying goes. But with Yuan's help I gained an advantage. He reserved the books he knew I'd need and let me borrow up to ten at a time, whereas other students were permitted to borrow only six.

Knowing how many volumes were waiting for me to read and how many assignments needed to be finished, I was forced to read and write very quickly. In order to have more time to study, I cancelled all my entertainment – no picnics, no shopping, no movies. When I wasn't attending classes, I spent most of my time in the library. Every day I got up at six in the morning and went to sleep at midnight. One thing I didn't cancel was exercise; the first thing I did every morning was to run about two thousand metres on the sports ground.

One morning when I was running, Huang, the coach of the university volleyball team, stopped me. 'I've been watching you for many days,' he said. 'You have good physical stamina. Would you like to join the university volleyball team?'

'Oh no, I can't.' I refused without thinking.

'Why not?'

'I don't think I'm qualified for it.' I used to like playing table tennis at school but I had seldom played volleyball.

'It doesn't matter, I'll train you,' Huang said kindly.

'Sorry, I don't want to trouble you. Besides, I have no spare time.' I explained my real reason. I knew it would take many hours away from my study.

'It won't take much time, only two hours a day in the late

afternoon,' he said persuasively. 'Besides, you can't study all the time. Sport is also good for your study.'

No matter how hard he persuaded, I still couldn't accept. And no matter how often I refused, Huang still tried to convince me, again and again. Every morning he waited for me on the sports ground, and then he'd talk while we ran.

One morning, two weeks after he first approached me, he ran with me as usual. 'Have you changed your mind?' He stopped and took a breath. 'The national competition for university students will be held in June this year. I really hope you will join the team and make a contribution for our university.'

His last words convinced me. Winning honour for the university was important to me. I couldn't say no any more.

That afternoon I put on the volleyball uniform and started playing. The first preliminary match would be held somewhere in Anhui province in April, in two months' time. There were twelve universities and colleges in Anhui, and the team ranked first would compete in the final in Qingdao, a beautiful seaside city in Shandong province.

Though I was the second tallest in the team, I was the worst player and I had to practise harder than the others. I was always exhausted afterwards and eager to lie on my back. I had to order myself to get up and go to dinner and on to another few hours of study. I was so tired that my eyes often closed against my will. I would have to put aside the law books to read aloud English texts, and continue my legal study when my head was clear. Then I found another method of staying awake – washing my face with cold water. In the spring it was still chilly in Hefei and because of this cold washing I got a cough and a runny nose. So I had to try another method: in ancient times, in order to study assiduously, people tied their hair to a beam to keep from nodding off, or prodded themselves with an awl in the thigh. I took to pinching my arms or legs whenever my eyes started to close. This was very helpful, but also painful.

Two months later, I had made much progress in my volleyball proficiency. Our team became the champion of the province, and in order to win the final, we were not allowed to relax. We didn't just practise every afternoon as usual, but also added an hour's practice early in the mornings. The university exempted us from the end-of-term examinations in July so that we could spend more time preparing for the finals.

So while other students were busy studying for their exams, we got on the train to Qingdao. We were unlucky in that the first match we played was against Beijing University, the future champions. We were too nervous to play well, and lost the match zero to three in twenty minutes. The second was against Shanghai's Fudan University, which ultimately won second place in the competition. We lost that match too.

After four days of play, my left leg felt sore whenever I moved it. I thought it must have been from overuse and did nothing about it, but the soreness increased when I returned to university. Before long I started to walk with a limp and the pain extended to the whole leg. The leaders of both the university and the department took my condition seriously and I was sent in the chancellor's car to all the big hospitals in Hefei, including the military hospital. Each one had its own opinion, and no hospital could give an exact diagnosis. They all said it was the first time they'd seen such symptoms and could offer no treatment.

My leg grew worse day by day. In a week's time, I wasn't able to walk, then I wasn't able to stand, and then the pain spread to my right leg. I had to stay in bed day and night, and could do nothing without help. My classmates looked after me in turns. This suffering, which had come all of a sudden, once again threw me into a bottomless chasm. I had an ill vision of my future: I would never stand up again, I was going to be paralysed. I wouldn't complete my university study and I would never be a judge.

During the day, not wanting my classmates to see my tears, I did my best to keep a smile on my face. But at night I couldn't control myself and wept bitterly. What would I do if I was unable to walk again? Let my parents take care of me all my life? What would be the use of living like that? I thought of suicide – at least that way I wouldn't trouble my parents. But I knew how sorrowful and disappointed they'd be. I couldn't be so selfish. I prayed to God in my heart: Don't be so cruel to me. I have a lot of things still unfinished. I haven't realised my dream yet. I haven't displayed filial piety towards my parents. I felt like my spirit had collapsed.

In the morning, the sun shone. It was another beautiful day but to my eyes there was only darkness, as dark as night. After breakfast, Professor Zhao came to see me. He was an English-language and literature professor and was in his sixties with short white hair. He was a kind and optimistic man, always cheerful and pleasant. Seeing my knitted brow, Professor Zhao smiled and tried to encourage me with a story about the Cultural Revolution. In those days, teachers were one of the targets of the proletarian dictatorship, and Zhao, along with other teachers, was regularly paraded through the streets with a big board hung around his neck and a pointed paper hat half a metre long on his head. Many teachers were beaten for refusing to wear the hat but Zhao didn't care and would put it on himself. While other teachers didn't feel like eating and sleeping, he had good meals and slept well.

'My life philosophy has been that a wise man doesn't fight against impossible odds,' he told me. 'As long as the green hills last, there will always be wood to burn. It has helped me endure years of suffering and deprivation, and I hope you can be optimistic about your future. Brace up! Everything will be fine.'

Teacher Li also came to console me. 'Even if you never walk again, you can still pursue your writing career,' he said. 'Do you remember that Russian writer whose most famous work was written when he was blind and paralysed?'

I understood my teachers' well-intentioned advice and I appreciated their goodness, but it was hard for me to do as they said. I didn't know what lay ahead or what my future would be. I asked the university to inform my parents and let me go back home. Maybe the doctors there could help me. It was my last hope.

Two days later, after more than a week in bed, I set off under the escort of three classmates, two kindly boys named Duan and Hou, and one warm-hearted girl named Sui. Other classmates, teachers and leaders came to bid me farewell as I was being driven to the station. The girls cried on each other's shoulders. They had the same thought as me – that I might not be coming back.

'You must return to attend the graduation examinations, even if you're lying in a stretcher,' one said.

'Don't worry about your study. We'll help you.'

'Take it easy. Let the university know whenever you need our help. Keep in touch.'

I was so moved I didn't know what to say, and just kept nodding my head.

There was one other person who was seriously upset, more upset than the rest, and that was my boyfriend Feng. We'd known each other since starting university. He was also studying English, and while we weren't always in the same classes we spent a lot of time studying together. We didn't make our feelings for each other known; in fact, most Chinese people at that time were shy about having their love relationships made public before marriage. On top of this, the university did not advocate its students have relationships in case it distracted them from their studies. So all love affairs were kept secret – there were no dates at the movies, or holding hands in the park, or other things that Western couples might do, and most of the time Feng and I spent together was in the library.

Even though he couldn't be forthcoming about the extent of his concern for me, Feng kept his worried eyes on me. As I was leaving he found a moment to slip a note into my hand, on a piece of paper folded into the shape of a bird. On the left wing were the words, 'Spring will not be far off since winter has come,' and on the right, 'I'm waiting for you to fly back like a bird.' I held it tightly, my eyes brimming with tears, trying not to let my emotions show.

Then I heard a burst of shouts behind me. 'Hope you recover quickly! Come back soon! See you in no time!' It was time to go.

The trip home was long and drawn out. We went by train to North Wuhu, a city by the Yangtze River, then crossed by ferry to South Wuhu and took the river boat to Jiujiang, nearly two hundred kilometres from Nanchang. In those years, public transport was impossibly crowded in China. Many people held tickets without seats. On trains they stood in the aisles, and during the peak season some had to stay in the toilet or lie under seats. On boats the decks were crammed. In order to get a seat, and space to put their luggage, people had to scramble to get on board.

Duan, one of my escorts, had a letter from the university which he gave to the head of the station, who agreed to give us special consideration. He allowed us to get on the train before everyone else, and let us take up five seats. I myself took up three of them because I could not bend my legs. Sui carried me on her back onto the train. When we arrived in Wuhu, we were again given special care, thanks to the letter from the university. Under the gaze of all the other passengers, I got on board the ferry and then the boat on Sui's back.

More than twenty hours later, the boat berthed at the dock of Jiujiang, where my parents picked me up. After saying thanks and goodbye to my three classmates, who returned by the same boat, I was taken to Nanchang in a van and sent directly to the city's best hospital. Four directors of the surgical departments from four major hospitals consulted regarding my illness, and after a two-hour examination and discussion, they finally gave a diagnosis – at midnight.

'She has sustained a severe injury to the great gluteal muscle, where the sciatic nerve passes,' the chief of the consultative group explained to my parents. 'An infection in the muscle has spread to the sciatic nerve, it's too painful to bear. The first thing we must do is stop the pain; we'll start treatment with a combination of traditional Chinese and Western medicine. But this is the first such case we have seen. We can't say if she will recover completely. Anyway, we'll do our best.'

After a few minutes, a nurse came to give me an injection and two tablets. She said the injection was for the pain and the tablets were for sleep. I hadn't had any relaxing sleep for two weeks, but that night my pain was a little reduced and I soon fell asleep. The next morning, I started the various treatments: physiotherapy, massage and acupuncture, and traditional Chinese herbs two or three times a day. These included pseudo-ginseng, musk, hairvein agrimony, the root of the herbaceous peony, and the root of the membranous milk vetch.

I felt anxious lying in bed all day long and thought constantly about my study. I asked my parents to bring me some books and papers and I made a new timetable for myself. In the mornings I did my law study, which I refused to give up until all hope was gone. In the afternoons I studied English as I didn't want to abandon my degree. In the evenings I kept a diary recording my thoughts and everything that had happened during the day.

Two weeks later, I felt much better, though I still had some pain. Twice a day I would stand up and try to walk with a pair of crutches. This improved my mood enormously – although I didn't know if or when I would walk unaided, I saw some hope.

The woman in the next room was surprised. 'How can you walk after only two weeks of treatment? And you look much fatter than before,' she said with admiration.

'I will let the doctors down if I don't get better,' I smiled. Actually, not even the doctors knew which of the treatments was helping me recover so quickly. 'As for looking fatter, that's because I've had hormone injections for my pain.'

She didn't believe this, and pressed my face gently with a finger. 'Oh, my god,' she laughed. 'I made a mistake. Your face is swollen!'

After three months of treatment and rest, I recovered completely, with no after-effects. The day I was allowed to leave hospital and return to university I didn't know how to express my excitement. I thought only people who escaped death by the skin of their teeth had such feelings as mine. I hurried to pack my things, I didn't want to stay one more minute in hospital. The doctors gave me a prescription and urged me to take the medicine on time, and not to take part in any physically demanding sports or labour.

'No words can express my gratitude,' I told them. 'You

haven't just helped me walk again, but have also given me a future.' I was so excited I could barely speak coherently.

My nextdoor neighbour came to say congratulations. 'I'm so glad for you. You look great now you're thin again. It's said that after surviving a great disaster, one is bound to have good fortune in later years. You must have a lucky future.'

I felt luckier than she was just then. Her leg had been broken in an accident and she'd had to have it reset three times. It still hadn't healed and she'd be staying on in hospital after I left.

'Thank you,' I told her, 'but I don't dare to expect good fortune, I shall be satisfied if it's not too bad.' I wondered whether I could bear it if disaster struck me again.

I went back to university in October. The new term had begun in September, and my teachers and classmates were greatly surprised to see me standing before them, and were eager to hear what had happened and whether I had completely recovered. The head of the department took great care of me, and let me decoct my medicinal herbs at her home, which was close to the university. Preparing these herbs was a time-consuming process and there were no facilities to do this in the dormitory.

Because I had missed so many classes, my first and most important task was to copy my classmates' notes. The Chinese method of teaching involved force-feeding texts to students. Teachers spent most of the class time explaining the texts word by word, sentence by sentence, paragraph by paragraph. If you wanted to get high marks in examinations, what you needed to do was take perfect notes in class and be able to regurgitate them. I borrowed the notes of a classmate and copied them page by page. My time was limited as I had much more work to do than the other students, making up not only for the missed lessons, but doing my legal studies as well. By that time I had studied several books on the basic theory of law, the history of Chinese law, civil law tenets, criminal law tenets, the theory of procedural law, an introduction to commercial law, as well as some case books. I had a fair understanding of law by then.

At the end of my third year at Anhui I wanted to gauge how I was progressing in my law studies, so Teacher Li got me a copy of the postgraduate law examination paper, the first such examination to be held since the Cultural Revolution. I completed the exam in my own time and Teacher Li then introduced me to Professor Zhou, a famous expert in civil law in China, explaining that I wanted to study postgraduate law. Professor Zhou was a very kind man and happy to help young people. He read my answers to the exam and then asked me some further questions. Finally, he smiled with satisfaction and declared that my answers were the best he'd received.

'What books have you read?' he asked me. I told him and he looked at me in wonder, saying he admired my talent and attitude to study and that I'd have no trouble entering the postgraduate course once I'd completed my degree.

I went into raptures at his words; I felt that the road to becoming a judge was underfoot. 'It would be a great honour to be your student,' I said.

Professor Zhou went on, 'As I am around seventy, I have a large collection of valuable law books which I've been thinking of passing on to a promising student. You might be the one.' He stopped for a moment. 'But I have a request: you must stay in the law department and work with me after graduation. One day you will be a professor too.'

I was struck dumb by this remark. I didn't want to study law in order to become a researcher or a professor. What should I do? It was impossible to accept his kind offer. Should I tell him I couldn't because I wanted to be a judge? It was difficult to respond without hurting him, so I said neither yes nor no but forced a smile.

In July 1982 I obtained my Bachelor of Arts degree but I did not go on to study postgraduate law. As the work of the law courts had expanded, there was a greater demand for legal people, and because there had been no graduates during the Cultural Revolution, it wasn't necessary to have a formal law qualification in order to work in the law courts. My father had a friend who was the director of the University Students Assignment Office for Jiangxi province. I wrote to ask him if he could assign me a job in a court – I did not want to ask my father to make this request for me – and he obliged by assigning me to the Nanchang Railway Transport Court.

His letter brought me great happiness but also great disappointment: it caused Feng to part company with me. His mother objected to our relationship, saying that it was difficult for a woman to satisfy both her career and her family at the same time. So if a woman had a strong career mind she would not be a good wife or daughter-in-law. And, traditionally, law was not an area in which Chinese women worked. Feng was the only child in his family and I understood how hard it was for him to please both his mother and his girlfriend. I didn't want to embarrass him by making him choose between us and so we said goodbye.

Even at this early stage, I felt I had paid a high price for my career, not only in losing Feng but in all the previous hardships. I hoped that my path would be smoother in the future.

初 到 法 院
THE FIRST TASK

I started work in the Nanchang Railway Transport Court on 20 August 1982 at seven-thirty in the morning. The first thing I saw when I got there was a big national emblem hung on the concrete wall over the gate. It showed Tiananmen Square and the five stars of the Chinese flag (representing prosperity), and it symbolised the organs of government. I felt excited at the thought of working in such a stately place and performing such solemn duties. I showed the entrance guard my order of appointment and he led me into the yard, pointing to a four-storey building. 'The personnel department is on the first floor,' he said.

I knocked on the door and the director of the department received me. Jiao was in his fifties, a tall northerner with a black face full of wrinkles who spoke with a Henan accent. He had served in the army for sixteen years and had then worked for the Railway Public Security Bureau for more than ten years, before transferring to the court. When the Chinese courts gradually began to return to normal after the Cultural Revolution, many police officers were transferred to work in them. Some old cadres who had been sent to the countryside for re-education were also reinstated.

Jiao asked me to sit down, passed me a cup of tea and said, 'Xiao Wang, from today you are a court cadre. There are several work disciplines a court cadre has to keep.' He gave me a booklet to read later and proceeded to brief me on the court system and structure. There were six divisions in the Railway Transport Court – the first criminal division, the second criminal division, the commercial division, the execution division, the personnel department and the administration office. There were fifty-two personnel, including judges, assistant judges, clerks, court police officers, archivists, legal medical experts and administration staff. The Railway Court tried cases that occurred in the Railway Bureau, which was responsible to the central government rather than the provincial government and was in charge of many work units, including factories which manufactured goods for the railway, construction companies, offices, as well as shops, hospitals, schools and cinemas for employees. It was like a suburb. If any crime was committed within that suburb, the case was tried in the Railway Court. And in any commercial legal cases where the defendant worked in a unit of the Railway Bureau, the matter was also heard in the Railway Court.

As was the case for all university graduates, I would be on a one-year training and probationary program, learning the work of a court clerk and judge. The court's Party committee had decided to assign me to the commercial division, whose chief judge was Judge Qi and who, like Jiao, had been in the Public

Security Bureau before coming to work in the court. When Jiao took me to meet him, he gave me a pile of books, including copies of all the relevant laws and regulations, and a case file. 'Read the file carefully,' he said, 'and then you'll learn from Xiao Xu what a clerk does. Later you'll learn the work of a judge. You should work hard,' he advised me.

'I will,' I promised him, and left. My office was next door on the third floor. There were four desks, which had been pushed together in pairs, and a pair of wooden sofas. My desk was by the window. Sitting facing me was Tu Ke, a middle-aged lady who wore a pair of terribly thick glasses. She spoke quickly, without pausing, and was a frank woman with a very warm heart – she became a good friend of mine. Xiao Xu sat near the door, and at the fourth desk was Xiao Cao, a short, thin young man who was the head of the Party group of our division. They were all clerks. I looked around the office; it was simple but clean and my colleagues looked friendly. I sat at my desk and said to myself, Good begun, half done. My career starts from today and here – I must make a good start.

Xiao Xu explained to me what a clerk did. 'Our main task is to take minutes of the conversations between the judge and clients. We must note down every sentence related to the case.' He indicated the case file that Judge Qi had given me. 'The defendant of this case will come at three o'clock. You need to go over the case quickly now and try your best to take the notes then.'

I spent over two hours reading the case file and getting an idea of what had happened between the two parties. I thought it would be no problem to note down the points of discussion, as my writing was faster than that of most of my classmates. But when the time came I felt a bit nervous as Judge Qi started his questions, and after writing for nearly two hours, barely raising my head, I had an ache in my right hand. I looked at my five pages of closely written characters, all in a mess, and understood that legal clerical work was not easy.

Compared with me, Xiao Xu had done a beautiful job. His notes were clear, tidy and complete. He passed them to the client and asked him to read them carefully for any mistakes.

The client asked Xiao Xu to amend only one sentence. Xiao Xu did so, then took out a small box of cinnabar and asked him to place his seal on the words that had been changed. For most of China's history, signatures have not been used (although this is changing now), and if someone did not have a personal seal, they had to use fingerprints instead. As the client did not have a seal, he dipped his thumb in the cinnabar and pressed it where Xiao Xu pointed on the page, and again on the bottom of each page to confirm that the notes were correct.

A few days later I got my all-important working card. It was in a little red plastic cover with the national emblem of China on it and contained a photo of me, my name, age and position, and my employer's details. The working card at that time was a formal means of identification, and was essential for obtaining a number of services, such as buying an air ticket, checking into a hotel and accessing the offices of government organisations.

Tu Ke smiled at me when I got my card. 'That shows you're working for an organ of the state,' she said. 'A lot of people want to be in such a place. You know, having a work unit in the Railway Bureau means having an iron rice bowl.' (Having a secure job, as solid as iron.) 'You're not only in a law court but in a railway court, which means double the security. Take my advice, don't ever leave here rashly.'

I knew that lots of young people wanted to work in a law court. And Tu Ke was right; working in a railway unit was considered to be as secure a job as working in a bank, which was regarded as a gold rice bowl, or in a post office – a silver rice bowl. But what Tu Ke didn't know was that I wanted to work in a law court not in order to have a secure job or to follow the fashion; I had my own pursuits and objectives, a struggle that she might not understand. I didn't say anything, merely returning an appreciative smile for her good intentions.

After several months of my training program, I felt I had a strong grasp of the processes of the Chinese legal system, which is vastly different to that of Western countries. Instead of a jury, China uses a panel of three judges, one of whom acts as the presiding judge and is appointed by the chief judge of the relevant division. The other two members are either judges or assistant judges. With the exception of simple civil and commercial cases, all cases are tried by such panels. In making a judgement, the three panel members' decisions have equal weight, with the majority ruling – it is not necessary to reach a unanimous decision. For major and difficult cases, final judgement lies with a judicial committee consisting of the president and vice-president of the court and the chief judges of each division. However, in practice the latter can override the panel's decision in any case where it does not agree with the judgement.

Whereas judges in most Western countries try cases by hearing the lawyers of the different parties examine the accused, victims and witnesses, Chinese judges also do a lot of investigative work, similar to that done by lawyers or police detectives in the West. Even though the Public Security Bureau will have established the facts and evidence of a case before it comes to a judge, the judge must confirm the facts on the basis of the evidence, and if they consider any details to be suspicious or unclear or inadequate, they must check those facts themselves. And during the court hearing, the judge in China is more actively involved in the proceedings, examining all those involved in the case. In a way, Chinese judges are like Western judges, lawyers and detectives rolled into one.

Defendants in China have the right to appoint their own lawyer to represent them, but in some civil or commercial cases, if a defendant cannot afford a lawyer they do without one. In the initial trial for criminal cases – but not in subsequent appeals – all defendants must have a lawyer, so if they cannot afford one, the court will appoint one for them. Chinese judges have little contact with lawyers while they're in the process of actually trying criminal cases, unless they need to check certain facts or the lawyer approaches them with new evidence. When trying commercial cases, however, Chinese judges are in much closer contact with the lawyers for both parties, as the preference is for settling such disputes through mediation rather than judgement.

But it is much easier for Chinese lawyers to have access to judges before and after cases than it is for Western lawyers.

One morning, as I was reading the file on a dispute over damaged goods, Judge Liu, the chief judge of the first criminal division, came to summon me to a meeting. Lin, the president of the Railway Court, wanted to see me. President Lin was nearly sixty, with a great deal of experience in handling criminals. He was a very serious person who spoke and smiled little. It was hard to know what he was thinking, and all the cadres in the court were afraid of him.

I stood just outside his office on the first floor and waited for him to ask me in. He sat before a big desk facing the door. 'Come in.' He waved his hand.

I entered and stood close to his desk. He didn't ask me to sit down but went on, 'I have a task for you. You've been receiving training in the duties of a clerk and a judge, haven't you? Now I'm going to give you the chance to find out what a court policewoman does. Tomorrow you'll go with a clerk and a court policeman to bring in a woman offender who is awaiting trial out of custody, since her offence is minor. Judge Liu will explain the details this afternoon.'

Every court had assigned to it a certain number of policemen and policewomen whose duties included guarding defendants during hearings, accompanying clerks when they delivered summonses and other legal documents, and accompanying judges while they interrogated criminal defendants. They were also responsible for court security during hearings. Where the defendant was a woman, a court policewoman was required.

As soon as I went back to my office, Xiao Cao and Tu Ke wanted to know why Chief Judge Liu had called me. I told them I was going to fill in as a court policewoman and bring in an offender from a small town in Hunan province.

'What? You collect an offender? That's Xiao Yan's work,' Tu Ke interrupted.

'Judge Liu said Xiao Yan suffers car sickness,' I said.

'Well, what does she do every day as a court policewoman, *chi bai fan* (do nothing but receive wages)?' Xiao Cao said.

From Tu Ke I learnt that Xiao Yan was the daughter-in-law of the vice-chief prosecutor of the Railway Public Prosecution Organ. She was one of those people who depended not on their capacities in order to enter a good work unit and get a good job, but on the influence of parents, relatives and friends – the back door, in other words. This was a common phenomenon in state organisations and companies: some people sat chatting in their offices while others worked themselves to death. But no matter what my attitude was on this matter, I was still pleased to have the chance to learn different things. Working was learning, and learning would enrich my knowledge.

Next day, with Xiao Chen – the clerk of the case – and Xiao Peng – a court policeman – I got on the train to Zhuzhou city in Hunan province, about seven hundred kilometres from Nanchang. The offender lived in a small town over a hundred kilometres further on in Chalin county. From Zhuzhou we took a long-distance bus and then a local bus.

It was four o'clock in the afternoon when we arrived. We contacted the town's Party secretary, explained our task and asked his assistance with arranging accommodation. There was no hotel in the town and only one long-distance bus a day. We couldn't leave until next morning. The Party Secretary had a woman open two guestrooms in the Town Hall for us. Xiao Chen and Xiao Peng shared one, and I took the other. It was the simplest room I had ever been in – nothing but a plank on two benches half a metre high, spread thickly with straw. A plain sheet covered this and there was also a quilt. That was all.

From there we went to the offender's home. The woman who opened the door was nearly as tall as I. Xiao Chen handed her the court subpoena.

'Ding Meihua, I give you formal notice of your court case which will be heard in four days' time. As a concealer of stolen goods, you must be present in court,' Xiao Chen explained. 'We will catch the bus at nine tomorrow morning. Be prepared for it. Do you understand?'

'Yes,' the woman answered.

'Do you have any questions?'

'Yes, please don't put handcuffs on me. Let me go to the bus stop myself.'

We looked at each other and agreed to her request. Later, on the way to a restaurant, I asked Xiao Chen what we would do if she ran away. Chen thought it wouldn't happen because the woman knew her crime was minor and wouldn't result in serious punishment. Furthermore, she would have escaped already if she had planned to do so. I hoped he was right.

I knew Hunan people liked hot food but I didn't expect every dish we ordered to be hot. Though we took out all the red chillies, which covered almost half the plate, the rest was still too hot to eat. I asked the waiter to bring me a big bowl of water, in which I rinsed every piece of meat, fish and vegetable before eating it. Even so, after finishing it I felt hungrier, as my heart was burning.

Next morning, we were at the bus stop ten minutes early. Ding Meihua arrived on time and we breathed a sigh of relief. We were about to get on the bus when Ding's mother-in-law appeared and made a tearful scene.

'Don't take her away, please!' She pulled at my arm. 'My family relies on her. If you must take someone, take me with you, since I can't live without her.' She repeated these words again and again.

More and more local people came to look on. I tried to remove the woman's hand from my arm but failed. She caught hold of me tightly, and I was afraid that if I pushed her away she would fall down. I had never had this experience before and didn't know how to deal with it.

'Let go, you can't do this. We're on official duties,' I explained to the old woman. But she seemed not to hear me.

'Loosen your grip, otherwise we will take you with us as well,' Xiao Peng shouted at her. His rude voice frightened her. She took her hands away and sat down on the ground, crying. The bus started as I jumped onto it.

At three in the afternoon, we arrived at the train station in Zhuzhou. We went to a noodle restaurant for lunch and Xiao Chen bought a meal for all of us, including Ding. She looked surprised and said, 'You are nice people, different from policemen.'

'How dare you say offensive words about policemen?' Xiao Peng stopped her. But I was soon to understand Ding's reaction to us only too well.

The train pulled into Nanchang station well after midnight. A prison van was waiting outside to take us to the detention house, where offenders awaiting judgement were kept. A guard opened the imposing iron gate and the van drove in and stopped in front of the office. Two policemen and a policewoman came out to receive us and Xiao Chen completed the transfer. Then the policewoman, tall and strong with round eyes and short straight hair, asked Ding and me to step into an inner room. A body search was required and two people needed to be present. 'Step forward!' the policewoman ordered rudely. Ding stood still by the wall and looked at me with scared eyes. I asked her quietly to obey the order, though I thought the policewoman's voice was too fierce – Ding was only a minor offender, after all.

'Take off your clothes!'

Ding, standing before the policewoman, looked very frightened and glanced at me again with puzzled eyes. I indicated that she should do as ordered. She took off her jacket and jumper.

'Go on!'

She went on, taking off her trousers. Now she wore only a T-shirt and pants and was shivering with cold. The policewoman picked up the jacket from the chair, searched it carefully and slowly, then put it back and searched the jumper. Ding was freezing and looked at me pleadingly. I didn't know if the policewoman had noticed or not and I couldn't understand why she didn't let Ding put her jacket back on since she had finished with it. Ding had to wait ten minutes before she was allowed to put on her clothes.

'What is in your bags?' The policewoman pointed to two cloth bags on the ground. 'Pass them to me.'

In one bag were peanuts and the other was filled with clothes, a toothbrush, and other articles for daily use. After checking them the policewoman threw them on the ground. 'No food is allowed to be brought in. We have to confiscate it.' She put the peanuts in another bag.

Still shivering, the offender was taken away.

It was nearly two o'clock in the morning when I left the detention house, glad I wasn't going to be a court policewoman.

死 刑 执 行

THE EXECUTION

On 2 September 1983 the Standing Committee of the National People's Congress – the Chinese parliament – announced a new movement known as *Yanda*. This movement aimed to crack down on those who were considered a threat to public safety, and allowed for more severe punishment of such criminals as hooligans, delinquents, those who intentionally caused grievous bodily harm to others, groups which forced women into prostitution or abducted them and sold them as wives, or which abducted young boys and sold them to families with no sons. This last was still a common occurrence in more remote areas of the country.

At midnight on 15 September the Public Security Bureau took sudden, coordinated action nationwide to detain more than a hundred thousand people suspected of being criminals, and sent them to local detention houses. There they were to be interrogated throughout the night and released if no criminal evidence was found within forty-eight hours.

Early the following morning, Aunt Bai, a friend of my mother's, called me on the phone. Aunt Bai wasn't my real aunt, but it's common in China to use this form of address with family friends. She was crying as she begged, 'Please help, please.' I asked her to calm down and tell me how I could help her.

'My daughter was taken away by the police last night,' she told me. 'I don't know why they arrested her. She's been in trouble in the past, but she has reformed herself and has done nothing illegal. Please help me to bring her back.'

I had heard of Aunt Bai's daughter. She was seventeen, and a year earlier had been ordered to do six months' reform labour for belonging to a delinquent gang. After that she had worked as a typist in a company and had stayed out of trouble. I couldn't understand why the police would have detained her either.

'Don't worry,' I comforted Aunt Bai. 'She'll be back very soon since she hasn't done anything wrong. I'll try to find out what happened.'

When I got to work I found all my colleagues talking about the huge wave of arrests the night before. I hurried into my office to make a phone call to a friend who worked in the Jiangxi Provincial Public Security Bureau. She told me that people with previous criminal records had also been detained but would all be released if they hadn't committed any fresh crimes.

Aunt Bai rang me again just as I was about to call her. Her voice had changed and she sounded excited. Her daughter was now safely back home and everything was all right.

Whereas it usually took three months for the prosecutor to undertake investigations and initiate public prosecution, and two months for the court to try the case, during *Yanda* this time was reduced by up to two-thirds. There was such a large increase in the volume of cases that something had to be done to speed up the processing of them. Four months after the new legislation had been introduced, forty criminals had been sentenced to death in the Nanchang area alone. They were all to be executed by shooting immediately following a joint public pronouncement of the judgement. All criminal judgements had to be announced in public, not only those that involved a death sentence, but usually pronouncements and executions were carried out individually.

On the day before the mass execution, Judge Liu, the chief judge of the criminal division, noted in a meeting that some ten people in the court hadn't attended an execution before and didn't know the procedure. 'These people should go tomorrow,' he announced, 'especially Wang Ling and Lao Zheng, as they may be directing executions in the future.'

Lao Zheng had just been transferred from the People's Liberation Army and had been appointed an assistant judge. As I had now finished my one-year training program, I had also been made an assistant judge, and at the start of *Yanda* I'd been assigned to the first criminal division to help with the increased workload. Every judge had to be trained in the use of firearms, something I had already done, but Judge Liu was right – I had never witnessed an execution. I had never even been to the execution ground, I had only seen the holes in the practice target. My only knowledge of the death sentence and its execution came from films and history books.

In imperial times the death penalty was commonly used in China and the means of execution were brutal. They included the Lingering Death, which involved cutting a person's flesh off piece by piece, sometimes in more than a thousand pieces; the Hot Pillar, whereby a person was tied to a hot copper pillar until they were charred; Dismemberment by Five Horses, in which the criminal's head and four limbs were tied separately to five horses, which were then ordered to run in different directions; and decapitation, after which the head was hung on a ten-metre-high tower over the city gate. In old times, the city gate was the only entrance and exit to the city, and people were forced to view the head of the criminal along with a notice about their crime.

The death sentence continued in modern China. General criminals were shot, but political criminals were often decapitated. Peng Pai, a famous leader of the Communist Party, was beheaded by the Guomindang soon after he was arrested during the War of Liberation. His head was hung up on the city wall and no one was allowed to take it down for two months. And shortly before the Communist Party came to power in 1949, two other important leaders of it were burnt to death in sulphuric acid.

On the morning of the execution day, I went with my colleagues to hear the pronouncement of judgement. There were thousands of voluntary spectators inside and outside the meeting hall of the court. In the yard and on the side road were dozens of open trucks, prison vans, cars, jeeps and three-wheeled motorcycles. At eight o'clock, eighty special armed police took the forty offenders into the hall and ordered them to stand on one side of the stage. The chief judge of the Higher Court of Jiangxi province read out the judgements, and notices of these were put up on the wall. The police then took all the convicted out to the trucks and prison vans and the procession set off, headed by four motorcycles. Bringing up the rear were the cars and jeeps in which sat the directors and supervisors of the execution. There were more motorcycles on each side of the trucks and vans to prevent them from being hijacked.

The execution ground was more than ten kilometres away from the city. There were many sentries posted along the way, and when we were getting close to the ground, I saw thousands of people waiting on the side of the road. Nearly a hundred policemen were guarding the only entrance. Following the other vehicles, we entered and got out in the centre of the ground. I looked around and saw a huge arena of more than two thousand square metres. Policemen stood shoulder by shoulder around the edge of it, forming a human wall. For safety reasons, the execution ground was about three metres lower than the road – it was also used as a military shooting range and was near a public thoroughfare.

Things happened quickly. In less than a minute all the convicted were lined up on their knees. The first shooters – members of the special armed police holding AK semi-automatic rifles – lined up a metre behind them. The directors and supervisors, second shooters and forensic experts stood behind them, and I was a few metres away, with dozens of other people from the Public Security Bureau, the Public Prosecution Organ and courts. As soon as the general director gave the order, I heard just one round of shooting and all the convicted fell down at more or less the same time. The first shooters then withdrew and the forensic experts and the second shooters stepped forward to check if there was anyone not dead.

One old woman – who had been convicted for abducting and selling eleven little boys to families without sons, two of whom had died – was found to be alive. She had fallen down before the bullet was fired. When the shooter turned her over, she sat up suddenly with terrified eyes, then knelt down again, begging to be spared. The shooter shot her at once, and as had happened with the others, her brains splattered out.

I felt terribly sick and turned back to the van. One by one the vehicles left the ground, while people from the funeral parlour put the bodies into plastic bags. When we reached the road, the sentries were withdrawing and the hearses were following our motorcade. The onlookers were gradually leaving. The whole execution had lasted only ten minutes, and everything went on as before as if nothing had happened.

According to traditional Chinese custom, those sentenced to death can eat and drink their fill before being executed, and those who attend can have a rich meal after it. But I had no such gourmet's luck; my mind was full of blood, brains and dead bodies. I felt nauseous all the way back to the city and didn't go to the restaurant with the others, but went straight to my office. I ate nothing at all for lunch that day.

After such a gruesome experience, I did not expect that just one year later, early in 1985, I would myself be directing an execution.

The convicted man was a rapist and the circumstances of

his crime were particularly serious. The primary court had sentenced him to death and his brother had then lodged an appeal on his behalf. I was a full judge by then and was appointed presiding judge of the legal panel. After reading the case files and questioning the witness and the offender, I determined that the accused had broken into the thirteen-year-old victim's home when her parents were absent. With a knife he forced the girl and her ten-year-old brother to stand at the side of the bed, and tied and gagged the brother. He then tied up the girl, who was shaking with fear, putting the knife into her mouth when she tried to scream. In front of her brother he took off the girl's clothes and raped her, hurting her badly and causing the onset of a mental disorder. In fact, she was so seriously disturbed I was unable to question her. The offender had admitted that this was the third time he had committed such a crime.

During our discussions, the three of us on the legal panel reached the same opinion and decided to affirm the original judgement. The offender had no further right of appeal, but I had to send the files with the judgement to the Higher Railway Court to approve the death sentence.

The execution was carried out two days later. I was the director of the execution as I was the presiding judge. This made me nervous, and a little scared. I did not sleep at all the night before the execution day – I could not forget the way the convicted man had stared at me with fierce eyes when I pronounced that the original judgement was to be allowed. Again and again I recalled his threat: 'I will remember you. I will repay you!' He repeated this as he was put in chains after I had finished the pronouncement. I asked myself many times if I had made the wrong judgement, whether it was possible to give him a chance to start his life afresh, but every time I answered no. He was guilty of the most heinous crime and his punishment complied with the law. I understood why he hated me so much, because I was his last chance, and he also thought I would be soft-hearted since I was a woman. But my duty was to punish crimes in accordance with the law, and the law was merciless.

After the pronouncement of judgement, I had gone with the two other judges and two court policemen to the detention house to verify the man's identity and take a final photo of him. I asked him if he had something he wanted me to tell his family. He took out his marriage certificate and passed it to me. He looked very peaceful then.

'Can you give this to my wife?' he asked. 'I wronged her. She is a good woman and she should have a good husband and a good future. I hope she will forget me and remarry.' His voice was low and serious. 'I'm sorry for my rude attitude to you. I don't hate you now, I understand you did your duty. I only hate myself. I'm guilty of an act that even death can't atone.' His eyes were full of repentance. I couldn't match him with the person who'd shouted at me in the courtroom earlier that morning and I couldn't help feeling pity for him. He might not have forfeited his life if he had repented and mended his ways earlier.

The pronouncement of judgement had been held in the hall of the City of Yingtan. Over a thousand people attended the meeting, and when I announced that the death sentence would be executed immediately, most of them rushed out of the hall and got on their bicycles to wait at the side of the road. As soon as our motorcade drove out, they followed closely after, blocking the traffic in the busy street. People on both sides of the road stopped to watch or joined the group on bicycles.

The execution ground was actually a piece of wasteland and one side of it was higher than the other. The onlookers were stopped by policemen on the higher ground and the condemned man was taken by two policemen to the lower ground and forced to kneel down, facing the onlookers. His arms were tied behind his back with a rope.

When I walked up to stand a few steps behind him, he turned his head and gave me a quick glance. I couldn't see his expression clearly and I didn't understand what his glance meant. I just stared at him and felt dizzy. I seemed to hear a voice in the distance: 'Why do you kill this person who has no enmity towards you?' And another voice at the same time: 'You are a judge. It's your responsibility to rid the people of an evil.'

'We're ready.' The chief judge was standing by, looking at me. I composed myself and saw the first shooter's gun already aimed at the convict. I hurried to give the order of execution.

The shot sounded but the convicted man still knelt, though there was a hole in his back. The whole ground was terribly quiet and everyone was looking in one direction – at the target. The people seemed to be as shocked as I was. I didn't know what I should do.

'The second shooter!' the chief judge ordered after more than ten seconds.

Just before the second shooter fired, the man turned and

fell, blood gushing from his chest. Another ten seconds later, he lay on his back with no expression on his face.

The whole scene felt like it happened in slow motion and it printed itself deeply in my mind. Around sixteen years have passed but I can still remember it as if it were yesterday.

法权较量

BETWEEN POWER AND LAW

The court system in China at that time consisted of the Supreme People's Court, the special courts and the local people's courts at different levels. There were three special courts: the Military Court, the Maritime Court, and the Railway Transport Court. Except for the Supreme Court, all the courts were composed of a higher, intermediate and primary court, which heard cases of varying degrees of seriousness. The courts at the primary and intermediate levels tried most cases in the first instance.

In the intermediate Railway Transport Court, my workplace, we heard appeals against judgements made in the primary court – lodged by either the defendant or the Public Prosecution Organ – and also conducted the initial trials for complex cases, such as those involving counter-revolutionaries, those in which there was a possibility of a sentence of life imprisonment or death, and those whose defendants were foreigners.

One morning in September of 1984, when I was still an assistant judge, I was proofreading a judgement with Huang, a young clerk just graduated from university, when Chief Judge Liu came to see me with a few files.

'How many cases are you handling at the moment?' he asked. Liu was actually one of two chief judges of the division.

'This one is almost finished.' I pointed to the written judgement. 'I have another two.'

'As you're familiar with the procedures for trying a case, I think you're capable of acting as a presiding judge now.' Presiding judges were appointed for each panel as the case arose. 'This is an appeal by a defendant. I have skimmed through the files and the circumstances are not complicated. Judge Shang and Judge Liao will be the other members of the panel.' He turned to Huang. 'You'll be the clerk.'

As he left the office, Liu urged, 'This is your first time in charge of a case. I hope you'll handle it well and finish it as quickly as possible.'

I was very excited. As an assistant judge, I'd been involved in previous cases only as a member of the panel, but now I was being asked to act as a presiding judge, where I'd be in charge of the panel and the case; I felt like I was now a real judge. Since so many cases were going through during *Yanda*, there were not enough judges to go round and assistant judges were sometimes made presiding judges.

I put aside my other files and opened the adjudication file from the primary Railway Transport Court. The most important line of the judgement leapt out at me straight away: '. . . sentence the two principal offenders Yu and Zou to death.' I started at the decision. I hadn't expected my first case as a presiding judge to involve the death penalty, and moreover the two defendants were boys aged just eighteen. I hurried to find the appeal petition presented by the second defendant, Zou, who had been convicted of resisting arrest and stabbing a man with a knife. He claimed that he hadn't stabbed anyone with his knife.

There were four files altogether for this case: two from the Railway Transport Public Security Bureau, one from the Public Prosecution Organ, and the adjudication file from the primary court. As this was an appeal, it was necessary to conduct a complete review of the facts, evidence and points of law applied in the trial. The fact that only one of the defendants had lodged an appeal did not affect the procedure – the entire case had to be reviewed. I started reading the two investigation files from the Public Security Bureau, which contained the records of interrogation, the testimony of witnesses, photos of material evidence, and the recommendation for prosecution.

The record of interrogation of the first defendant, Yu, read:

Public Security Officer You should know that our Party's policy is leniency to those who confess their crimes and severity to those who refuse. What do you want, leniency or severity?
Yu I want leniency.
PSO Very well then, make a clean breast of your crimes.
Yu On the afternoon of 25 August I went to ask Zou to play mahjong. He said he wasn't able to as he hadn't any money. [In China, mahjong is often played as a gambling game.] So I suggested that we go to Yingtan [a small town near the defendants' hometown] to find some cash. He agreed but said we'd better get one more person to go with us. Because it was our first time, he was scared. We asked

my neighbour Hong. He didn't want to come, until we promised him that all he had to do was be a guard for us.

At five o'clock we caught the train to Yingtan station. There were many people in the station square, and some railway policemen and security guards were walking around. I didn't think it was a good place, so we went to the public toilet on a corner of the square, close to the street. I asked Hong to stand outside and keep watch while Zou and I went in.

There were only two people inside. We pretended to piss until one man went out, then I took out my knife and stood to the left of the remaining man, who was squatting over the toilet. Zou stood to his right, a knife in hand too. [In provincial China, most public toilets consist of a long ditch separated into compartments by walls about a metre high, without doors.] I ordered the man to give us all his money. He looked very frightened and gave us his wallet. I took out all the cash – a hundred and seventy yuan. I left ten yuan for him and put the rest in my pocket. Then we ran out of the toilet.

Before we could run very far, the man rushed out shouting. People were running toward us from all directions but I was too scared to run quickly. I was soon caught and taken to the police station. Hong was already there, and after about twenty minutes Zou was also pushed in. This is all that happened. Not a word is false.

PSO How did you hold the knife when you asked the victim to give you his money?

Yu	My knife was pointed at the man. (*demonstrates*)
PSO	Do you know what crime you have committed?
Yu	Yes, robbery.
PSO	It's armed robbery. That's a serious crime.

The records of interrogation of the other two defendants, and the testimony of all the witnesses, proved the three defendants had committed the robbery, but I had a few important questions. There was a discrepancy in the record of the interrogation of the second defendant, Zou:

PSO	Did you hold your knife when you were escaping?
Zou	Yes.
PSO	What for?
Zou	I don't understand you. I had been holding the knife.
PSO	Why did you resist arrest?
Zou	I was frightened of being jailed.
PSO	So you stabbed a pursuer.
Zou	No, I didn't.
PSO	Well, where did the hole in the right sleeve of the security guard Zhang come from?
Zou	I don't know.
PSO	You don't want to confess your crime honestly, do you?
Zou	You can't force me to confess what I didn't do.
PSO	It doesn't matter if you don't confess. We have evidence.

The testimony of Zhang, the security guard of the train station, read:

> I was on patrol when I heard a man shouting in the direction of the toilet. Then I saw a man running out of the toilet. He shouted, 'Stop them! They stole my money!' I ran fast to catch up with him and asked who had robbed him. He pointed to three people running in front of us. I pursued them and asked them to stop but they didn't.
>
> Soon they ran in different directions. I followed one of them closely. He ran as fast as a rabbit, so I was a few metres behind him. I don't know how long we ran for. My legs felt like jelly and my throat was parched, but I didn't stop to rest even for a second. I thought I couldn't let the criminal escape.
>
> Suddenly he fell down. I dashed to him and seized him, but he resisted arrest and stabbed me with a knife. Fortunately, he didn't hurt me but stabbed through my right sleeve. At this point some other people came up to help me.

The testimony of Pang, a railway policeman, read:

> I heard people shouting, 'Stop them! Stop them!' when I was in the office. I rushed out and ran with some other people. They told me a man had been robbed. I ran as fast as I could and saw a young man running to a small lane with a knife in his right hand. I am very familiar with the district around the station because I have been working there for eight years. I took a short cut to block the way of the criminal. I shouted to him, 'Stop! Drop your weapon!'

He didn't obey me but turned back, trying to escape. This time Zhang, a security guard, and some other people came up. The criminal waved his knife and resisted arrest. I suddenly threw myself on him, holding his waist from behind. Then Zhang and some other people helped me to restrain him.

The testimony of Lu, a resident, read:

My girlfriend and I came to buy train tickets. I heard people shouting, 'Stop! Stop!' Then some people passed by us, running to the street. Without thinking, I left my girlfriend and ran after them. I'm a good runner and I won a lot of prizes in high school. Before long I caught up with the leader of the runners.

Suddenly the criminal fell down, and a man and I pounced on him. I took his knife away, then a policeman came to put handcuffs on him.

The testimony of Xu, another resident, read:

My home is near the place where the criminal was caught. I went out to see what was happening as I had heard a lot of noise outside. A few metres from my door, some people were grappling with a young man who was covered in mud. I saw a policeman put handcuffs on him. They pushed him forward. When they passed by me, more policemen came.

In the opinion of the Public Security Bureau:

> Although the defendant Zou was only an accomplice to the robbery, he resisted arrest by stabbing a pursuer with a knife. This offence is very serious, and he should be given as heavy a punishment as the first principal offender.

After two days of reading, I was puzzled by the different testimonies of the witnesses and could not understand how the Public Security had reached its conclusion. The Public Prosecution Organ had agreed with that conclusion, and it had also been confirmed by the panel of judges. The fact that Zou was considered to have resisted arrest was given as just reason for his death sentence. By then I understood that this was not a simple case of appeal – a young man's life was at stake. I had a grave responsibility, and I needed to investigate the dubious points and find out the facts for myself.

The next day, I passed on the files and my detailed reading notes to the other two members of the panel, Judge Shang and Judge Liao. I had an outline of interrogation prepared and asked Huang to go with me to Yingtan.

It took us more than three hours to get there by train and we went direct to the primary court. I wanted to talk first with the original presiding judge of the case, but he appeared displeased when he heard the purpose of my visit.

'I have handled so many cases, how can I remember such a small thing? I advise you not to spend too much time on it. It's a waste of time.'

I was taken aback. 'I don't agree. It's not a small thing, it concerns a person's life. I only want to know on what basis you confirmed that the second defendant Zou had resisted arrest by stabbing a pursuer. You may have noticed that each witness gave a different testimony. How did you decide which was the truth and should be used as evidence?'

'How dare you talk to me like this?' he exploded. 'I have crossed more bridges than the roads you have walked. Trust my experience, nothing is wrong. Furthermore, the final decision was made by the judicial committee of the court.' And with that he left.

I was not too surprised at this. I went next to the office of the chief judge of the criminal division.

'I want to interrogate the second defendant Zou,' I said, after explaining what I had come for. 'Can you assign a court policeman to come with us? And I also want to question the witnesses. I hope you can arrange this for me.'

'Since you are so serious, we have to assist you. How about tomorrow?' But I could feel his displeasure, even though he had so readily agreed.

At nine o'clock the next morning, we went back to the court where I was told that no court policeman would be available until the afternoon. I couldn't wait, I was too anxious to find out the facts. 'Let's go by ourselves,' I said to Huang.

'I have a feeling you've come up against a hard case and you'd better be mentally prepared,' Huang said on our way to the detention house. 'I don't know if you've realised that.'

'Yes, I have. But I don't care. I'm acting according to the law.' I was trying to convince myself as well as Huang.

'What will you do if there is really not enough evidence to prove that Zou resisted arrest by stabbing the security guard?'

'I'll revise the judgement of the first trial,' I said firmly. 'What's your opinion?'

'I'd do the same if I were you.'

Fifteen minutes later, I was interrogating the offender Zou in the detention house.

Contrary to my imagination, Zou was short and thin. He looked as though he were in shock at his circumstances, for his face was as pale as a sheet and he had a dull look in his eyes. He walked very slowly since he was in handcuffs and fetters.

'Sit down,' I said when he came in.

'Are you the appeal judge?' He looked surprised to see me.

'Yes,' I said. 'I'm the presiding judge. I'll be reviewing the whole case. Now, I have some questions. You should tell me the truth,' I warned.

'I will. But I didn't expect you to be so young, or a woman,' Zou murmured.

'Perhaps you don't trust me?'

'Yes, I trust you,' he said quickly, then grew excited. 'I hope you will be perceptive of the minutest details. I didn't stab anyone. You can't kill me!'

'Calm down. I will respect the facts and the law. I'll let them decide whether or not you will be killed,' I said. 'Sit down and answer my questions.'

He sat down slowly, eyes darting around the cell, and went on murmuring, 'I was wrongly accused. I didn't stab him.'

'Give me a detailed description of your arrest.'

'I was afraid of being arrested. That's why I ran and ran. Sometimes I took a look behind and saw a few people running after me. Suddenly I stumbled over the root of a tree and I fell. A man in army uniform without a collar badge tried to seize me. I hurried to jump up, trying to escape, and then a policeman approached from another direction. I was scared, so I waved my knife at the people who were blocking my way. They didn't give way but grabbed hold of me. That's all.'

'Who was the first person to seize you?'

'I can't remember. It seemed to be all of them, including the policeman.'

'How did you hold the knife and how did you wave it? Show me.'

'The point was to the front, the handle towards the back, and the edge down. Like this.' Zou gestured. 'I waved it left and right.'

'What else do you want to tell me?'

'No more. I swear what I've said is the whole truth.'

It was near midday when we left the detention house to return to the court. The chief judge told me he had arranged for the witnesses to come in that afternoon. He gave me a list of four people and said they were the only witnesses who had been found. At one-thirty I started to question the first of them, Zhang, the security guard. He was about twenty-five years old, of medium height, in a green army uniform.

'You must like the army uniform very much,' I smiled. In

those years, many young people were keen on army uniforms, it was the fashion.

'Yes. My brother is in the People's Liberation Army,' he said proudly.

'Do you remember the robbery which happened in the toilet near the train station?' I asked.

'Yes, I can remember every detail.'

'Good. I have some questions to ask and I hope you will tell me the truth.'

'Of course I will.'

'I want to know whether the defendant Zou stabbed you or not.' I caught his eyes and asked the key question straight away.

'Yes, he did. I have said so many times to the Public Security Bureau, the Public Prosecution Organ and your primary court.' He quickly moved his eyes away.

'Can you tell me how the defendant held the knife and how he stabbed you?'

'He held it in his right hand. The point was ahead and the edge down.'

'When did he stab you?'

'When I had both hands on his back, trying to pull him up – he jumped up and turned round to stab me.'

'How did he stab you?'

'Like this.' He gestured.

'Where did he hurt you?'

'He didn't hurt me, he just stabbed through my right sleeve, just above the cuff.'

'You mean, he stabbed you with the edge of the knife facing down, and he didn't hurt you but stabbed through your right sleeve, making two holes in it. Is that right?' I kept my eyes on his face.

'Yes. Oh no. I can't remember clearly.' His face started reddening. 'The edge of the knife was towards the right, no, left.' No, no, it was facing down.'

'How wide was your sleeve?'

'About seven inches.'

'Okay. You can leave now.'

I then separately questioned the other three witnesses. Their statements still didn't prove that Zou had stabbed Zhang, but I had a fair idea by then of what had really happened.

'We can catch the evening train back to Nanchang,' I said to Huang when I'd finished interviewing.

'Are we done here?' Huang was puzzled.

'Yes. I've got what I need. I'll show you tomorrow.'

It was eleven-thirty when I got home. My parents and sisters had already gone to bed, but my mother woke up, surprised to see me back so soon.

'Is everything all right?' She looked concerned. 'You have to be careful, you can't make even a little mistake.'

'I know.' I went to my room and sat down at my desk.

My mother knew I would stay up late again. She put a small plate of biscuits and a cup of tea on the corner of my desk and left quietly.

After going over my interrogation notes, I wrote a report in which I confirmed that the defendants had indeed committed the crime of robbery, as had been proved by the testimony of a witness, the statement of the victim, the statement of the defendants, as well as material evidence. But as to the circumstances of Zou stabbing his pursuer Zhang, I expressed a different opinion. We had only Zhang's statement to this effect, with no other evidence or proof, and his statement had an error in logic. He stated that Zou had held the knife with the point facing ahead, the handle towards the back and the edge facing down, and this was confirmed by the witnesses Pang and Lu and by Zou himself. But the holes in Zhang's sleeve were not consistent with this account. I suspected Zhang of putting them there himself, in order to prove his bravery. Since it could not be proved that Zou stabbed Zhang, we could not impose the death sentence. In accordance with the relevant items of criminal law and the decision of the Standing Committee of the National Congress regarding punishment of those seriously endangering public security, I recommended revising the original judgement and sentencing the defendants Yu and Zou to twenty years' imprisonment.

The next morning, I showed Huang my report and told him to ask Shang and Liao to attend a meeting of the panel.

'It's Zou's good luck to have you as the presiding judge of his appeal. Otherwise . . .' Huang made a shooting action.

'Don't speak too soon. I'm not so sure I'll win out.' I thought of what the chief judge had said when he gave me the case.

In the meeting, I told Shang and Liao what I had done and what my opinion was. They read through the interrogation notes quickly, then examined the knife and Zhang's clothes.

'I was a bit confused when I first read the file,' Liao said. 'Now it's very clear that the security guard didn't tell the truth. He wanted to prove his own bravery, as did some other witnesses as well. I completely agree with your recommendation to revise the judgement.'

'What do you think?' I asked Shang, who was keeping silent.

'I think this case was originally simple but it has been complicated by the testimonies. I agree it's unproven that the second defendant stabbed his pursuer, but it's a fact he resisted arrest. So I'm not sure if we need to revise the judgement, since the central government now stresses severe penalties.'

'I don't think severe penalty means we can give judgement beyond the law,' I argued.

Liao supported me. 'Xiao Wang is right. I think twenty years' imprisonment is severe enough for the defendants.'

'Okay,' Shang agreed grudgingly. 'Since you two have decided to revise the decision, I'm in the minority. So I have to submit.'

Each court in China has a judicial committee, consisting of the president of the court and the head judges of the divisions, which is responsible for reviewing difficult cases. Since our judges' panel could not agree on a decision, President Lin called a meeting of the judicial committee three days later. Huang and I also attended, and I gave a detailed account of the case and presented the material evidence. I then expressed my own opinion as to the judgement and the opinion of the other members of the panel.

There was an extended and terrible silence. President Lin kept drinking his tea, the vice-president and Chief Judge Liu kept smoking, and the others kept their eyes on the files.

A phone call suddenly broke the silence. President Lin answered it. 'Yes, speaking. We are discussing the case at this very moment. Ah, ah, severe punishment does comply with the decision of the central government. Don't worry, just go ahead with your work.'

'He's talking about this case,' Huang whispered. I nodded in agreement.

Lin hung up and turned to everyone. 'We'll take a break now. You can have time to think about this carefully. The meeting will start again in ten minutes.'

From what Lin had said on the phone, I had a feeling that a contest between power and law lay ahead. But I believed that I was right, and that both the facts and the law stood by me. I did not believe that power was still bigger than law in 1980s China.

'Do you feel something?' I asked Huang when the others had left the meeting room.

'Of course. You may lose the case.'

'No, I won't. I will win, though it will be hard,' I replied confidently.

'I hope so. But . . .'

'Will you support me? You know what that support means.' I was concerned that Huang might be putting his own future in the court in danger.

'Yes, I'll stand by you.'

'I just want you to do your best to take down every word then. That's it.'

'So simple?'

'Not so simple. It's very important to –' The others returned before I could finish. Huang gave me an understanding smile.

After everyone had taken their places, Chief Judge Liu expressed his opinion. 'Xiao Wang has done a careful investigation. It seems that there is not enough evidence to prove that the defendant Zou stabbed his pursuer. However, I don't agree that we should revise the original judgement. The three defendants committed armed robbery in a public place – this pertains to the crime of seriously endangering public security, and, especially during this period of *Yanda,* such actions should be taken more seriously. I think that if we sentence such criminals to death, it will be a lesson to others who are walking the edge of crime.'

I could not contain myself. 'Since it cannot be proved that Zou committed the crime of which he has been accused, the death sentence is obviously too severe. Furthermore, I think the punishment is too heavy for the other defendants in the case,' I retorted.

'Xiao Wang, don't forget that now is *Yanda.*' Liu raised his voice.

'I haven't. But *Yanda* must also comply with the law.'

Liu lost his temper. 'You may not understand what *Yanda* means. It means that too heavy a punishment is better than too light a one. We may be called left deviationists if we punish criminals too heavily, but we will be called right deviationists if we punish them too lightly. The former is a mistake in working method, but the latter is a mistake in thought and attitude.'

The other members of the meeting chimed in to agree with him.

'Chief Judge Liu is right. We can't let others say we have committed an error of thought.'

'We'd better affirm the original judgement. The less trouble, the better.'

'It won't be a pity to kill one more from such dregs of society. And we don't want to upset the original judges, or disturb the relationship between the primary court and our court.'

My body was shaking all over. I could control myself no more. I stood up and spoke loudly. 'We are judges. We hold power over people's life and death. We can not abuse this power. We must not use this power in accordance with our own will or interests, but must consider the facts and the law.' The more excited I got, the more I wanted to say. 'I hope –'

'You are too conceited!' Liu interrupted me. 'How can you accuse us of abusing power?'

'I –' I still wanted to argue but President Lin stopped me.

'That's enough. I have heard and understood everyone's opinion. My own opinion is that the judgement made by the primary court is a little heavy, but not improper. Taking into account the feelings of our comrades in the primary court, I agree with the majority, affirming the original judgement.'

I was so disappointed that my eyes were brimming with

tears. In order that this not be seen by others, I bent my head while President Lin was speaking.

'Xiao Wang, do you have any questions?' The president turned to me.

'According to the law, I have to obey the decision of the judicial committee, but I reserve my personal opinion,' I replied firmly.

'You will not put your differing opinion in your report on the case's conclusion,' Chief Judge Liu commanded.

The report on the case's conclusion was a legal document written by the presiding judge and this, together with my reading notes and report on the examination of the case, would be put into the internal adjudication file. Lawyers were not allowed to read the internal file, only the external file, which included the testimonies of witnesses, statements of defendants, records of interrogation and the hearing, as well as the judgement. While the judgement made after the appeal was final and a defendant had no further right of appeal, in the case of death sentences the written judgement and all relevant files – including the internal file – had to be submitted to the Higher Court for a procedure known as the review of death sentence. This was why I had asked Huang to take particular care in recording everyone's exact comments – so that the judge in charge of the review could see that there were differing opinions on the case.

Returning to my office, I checked the notes Huang had taken. They were absolutely complete.

'What do you think?' he asked.

'Thank you. They're perfect. I think I can win with such strong help from you.' I firmly believed that the judges in the higher court would properly consider the facts and the law.

'Will you obey Liu's order? I mean, will you put your own opinion in the file?' Huang asked.

'What do you think I'm going to do?'

'I think,' Huang wagged his head, 'the best way of dealing with an order from those who abuse their power is to defy it.' We both laughed.

But I knew that the review of the higher court was my last hope. I wrote my report paying careful attention to detail, and I relaxed a little when I saw Huang put it, together with his perfect minutes of the meeting, in the internal file.

Very soon I faced a terrible fact. As the presiding judge of the case, I had to put my name to the written judgement affirming the original judgement. And even though the review of death sentence had not been completed, I still had to pronounce the appeal judgement in public.

The meeting of pronouncement took place in the afternoon a week later. There were over a hundred people present, and the three defendants were taken to the corner of the stage. Chief Judge Liu declared the meeting open and I walked to the centre of the stage with a heavy heart. Against my will I pronounced the judgement. As soon as I read, 'The court has decided to reject the appeal and affirm the original judgement,' Zou fainted. I don't know how he was taken away. I don't know how I finished the pronouncement or how I left the stage.

One hour later, Huang went to the detention house to

deliver the written judgement. This was not my job but I went with him anyway, not knowing why. When I saw Zou again he glanced at me, whether with disappointment, bitterness, hatred or contempt I could not tell. Maybe it was all four. I wanted to tell him that the final judgement was not my own. I wanted to tell him I had done all I could to give him a fair judgement. I wanted to say I would still strive to do that. But I said nothing. I could say nothing – I was a judge, not his lawyer.

One afternoon about two weeks later, as I was going to the courtroom, a judge of the Higher Court rang me from Beijing. Judge Jiang told me he was in charge of the review, had noted my differing opinion on the judgement, and that he would be going to Yingtan to further investigate the case. Judge Jiang had more than twenty years' experience in judicial work, and I had heard that he was upright, honest and frank. I rejoiced inwardly.

Soon after, Judge Jiang spent two days in Yingtan before coming to our court to exchange opinions with Chief Judge Liu. He came to my office before he left for Beijing.

'Xiao Wang, you have done very well. I have told Chief Judge Liu my decision –'

'You mean you will revise the original judgement?' I interrupted.

'Of course I will. The only basis we should judge on is the facts and the law.'

I could hardly believe it. At last the contest between power and law had finished. The defendants had obtained a fair judgement. Instead of the death sentence, the first and second defendants, Yu and Zou, were sentenced to twenty years' imprisonment, and the third was sentenced to ten years instead of the original twenty. This case was the first in the Railway Court to have a death sentence overturned by the Higher Court. The news spread quickly and almost everyone talked about the matter, and about me.

A few days later, Judge Song, an old judge, came to my office. 'Xiao Wang, you really are audacious in the extreme,' he said. 'How dare you offend the president and the chief judge of your division?'

'Newborn calves are not afraid of tigers,' Huang said in fun.

'I didn't set out to offend anyone,' I said. 'I only did what I should.'

Judge Song shook his head. 'It's not worth doing so for a criminal.'

'No, it's more for the prestige of the law,' I corrected.

'You should know that the law is made by the people, and sometimes people's power is bigger than the law.'

'Not in my heart,' I persisted.

Xiao Wu, a young clerk, was worried about me. 'I heard that Lin and Liu have flown into a rage. I'm afraid you'll have a hard time from now on. Also you, Xiao Huang.'

'What can they do to me? Dismiss me? It's now the 1980s.' I thought of my father's misfortune, convinced that such a thing could never happen to me.

'Who cares? If that happens, we can go to Shenzhen,' Xiao

Huang said confidently. 'They need people there with knowledge of the law.'

'It will be your good luck if you're asked to leave,' Judge Song declared. 'I'm afraid if you are not, that will be worse.'

'I don't understand. What do you mean?' I asked.

'You'll understand soon enough,' he muttered.

Just then Liu came into the office. 'Xiao Wang and Xiao Huang, listen. A case of murder will open the court session tomorrow afternoon in Fuzhou. We'll catch the train at five-thirty this afternoon. Don't be late.' He put a few files on Xiao Huang's desk and ordered, 'Take these files with you.'

I glanced at my watch. It was already four-fifty. 'He should have notified me earlier,' I complained when Liu had left.

'It has begun,' Judge Song said.

'What has?'

'Retaliation.' Judge Song lowered his voice. 'You'd better be careful.'

Yes, I would have to be very careful. I remembered my grandmother once saying that, while you shouldn't harm others, you should take precautions against harm from others. Would I be able to guard myself? I had no time to think more about it.

进退两难
IN A DILEMMA

I had two phone calls to make before I left for Fuzhou. One was to my mother and the other was to my new boyfriend, Xiao Zhao, who was a schoolmate from high school.

Xiao Zhao and I had been in the same grade but hadn't talked much, though we were both cadres in the student union and often met in meetings. We hadn't had any contact after graduation until, by chance, we had met on a train six months before. It took me a few minutes to remember who he was when he called out to me, but we quickly caught up on old times. He had been in the countryside for three years after high school, and in 1977 had gone to Shanghai's Fudan University to study international finance. After four years of study he had been assigned to the Finance Bureau of Jiangxi province, as assistant to the director.

During our train conversation, Xiao Zhao confessed he had loved me since high school. He had known I was working in the court but was too shy to contact me and let me know his feelings. I was moved by his affection. He believed it was Heaven that had arranged this meeting, giving him the opportunity to pour out the words that had been hidden in his heart for ten years. Since that chance encounter, we'd seen a lot of each other; we met once a week, usually in the city library, and sometimes we went to see a film. But because of my heavy workload, I often had to cancel arrangements with him and this upset him a great deal.

And now, once again, I would have to cancel at the last minute. I dialled his number at work, but before I could ask to speak to him I was cut off. 'You'll have to ring back later, we're having a meeting right now,' a rude male voice said, and he hung up the phone.

I dialled again and the same thing happened. 'I told you to ring later,' and the phone went dead. I felt bad. Not only was I cancelling on Xiao Zhao, but I was leaving without saying a word.

I gave up and rang my mother's office, telling her I was leaving for Fuzhou in twenty minutes and would be back in a few days.

'Why are you in such a hurry?' my mother asked anxiously. 'Don't you have time to collect some clothes? The broadcast said the weather will be changing, it's going to be cold for the next few days.'

'Don't worry, I'll be fine,' I comforted her. 'I have to go. Bye.' With Xiao Huang, I ran all the way to the train station, which fortunately was not far from our office.

We arrived at Fuzhou, the capital of Fujian province, late the next morning. I had slept badly, even though we were in a sleeping car. I was thinking about Zhao all night, wondering how he'd felt when I hadn't shown up, when I hadn't even rung him. How would I be able to make him understand this time? I knew what he needed was for me to promise not to cancel any more arrangements with him, but how could I promise that? Last time, he'd complained, 'I understand that you love your career, I don't object to that, but would you please let me share some of it? You can't always put your career first, I don't know whether you love me or not.'

I made up my mind to call as soon as we got to our accommodation, but Liu was ahead of me. 'Hurry up, Xiao Wang,' he shouted, 'time for the meeting of the panel.' I had no choice but to follow him to the meeting, which lasted nearly two hours. By then there was no time to make a call before the court session began.

So it was after the court had closed before I could ring Xiao Zhao. Unexpectedly, he didn't appear to mind at all. 'When will you be back?' he asked.

'I'm not sure. Maybe the day after tomorrow.' I felt strangely bothered by his attitude. 'I'm sorry, I –'

'Can you call me as soon as you get back?' He didn't seem to hear me.

'I will.' But I could still feel his bad mood. 'Are you all right?'

'Let's talk when you're back.' He rang off.

I didn't understand what he wanted to say to me when I got back that he couldn't say on the phone. From his unusual attitude, I felt it must be a serious matter. And the only serious matter between us was our relationship. Was he going to say goodbye to me? My mind was all in a tangle. I stopped myself thinking about it and concentrated on my work.

'Xiao Wang, you draft the judgement of the case,' Chief Judge Liu ordered. 'More practice will be helpful to you.'

Actually it was Liu who should have been drafting the judgement, as he was the presiding judge of the case. But of course he was also the chief judge and had the power to order me to do it for him. I not only had to obey, I had to be grateful to him for giving me such an opportunity.

The next afternoon, I submitted to Liu the judgement I had written. One hour later, he returned it to me. To my surprise, my draft had been revised beyond recognition. I couldn't believe my writing was so terrible, and read it through carefully and patiently. After I'd finished, I couldn't help laughing.

'What's so funny?' Xiao Huang and Judge Geng, another member of the panel, took it and read it aloud. They too roared with laughter.

'Do you know why he did this? He has to make good use of the power he has now because he won't have it when he retires,' Xiao Huang ridiculed. 'Look, he's changed almost every sentence.'

'It's unbelievable. I've never seen anything like this before.' Judge Geng knitted his brows, pointing to the draft. 'Such good sentences have been changed to babble and disconnected phrases.'

'The most serious problem is that he has used incorrect legal phrases.' I couldn't believe he had confused the phrase of *cong zhong chu fa* (giving a heavier punishment within the maximum prescribed) with *jia zhong chu fa* (giving a punishment beyond the maximum prescribed). There was a huge difference between these concepts, but I knew Liu had confused them on purpose because he was determined to make things difficult for me.

'I think you should return the judgement to him and tell him you don't need such practice,' Xiao Huang suggested. 'Otherwise he will hound you endlessly.'

'No, she can't,' Judge Geng said. 'If she does, Liu will put a political label on her, claiming she has resentment against *Yanda*.' He turned to me. 'I think what you should do is amend the sentences as he's marked them. Don't forget that the name on the judgement will not be yours, but his.'

'You're right,' I said. 'But first I must point out to him the places that have legal mistakes.'

When I showed Liu the amended draft, he said, 'See, now this is much better.'

'But I didn't change *cong zhong chu fa* to *jia zhong chu fa*, because they have a different meaning,' I said carefully.

'Oh, I know.' A displeased look settled on his face. 'Leave it here. I'll do the final corrections.' And with that I left.

We returned to Nanchang on Saturday morning. Xiao Zhao didn't meet me at the station, although I had called him before I got on the train. I thought he might be really angry with me this time, so instead of going home I went straight to his house.

I knocked on the door but no one answered. I was turning to go when Xiao Zhao and his mother arrived. He was surprised to see me. 'Didn't you say you would be back tomorrow?'

I didn't answer him, just gave him a sweet smile and said hello to his mother first, as good manners dictated.

'It's good you've come back.' She opened the door and let me in. 'I have something to say to you.'

When his mother had gone to the kitchen to get the thermos for tea, Xiao Zhao sat beside me and said, 'I'm sorry. I mixed up the date of your return; I've been muddle-headed these days.'

'Is there something wrong?'

'Yes,' Xiao Zhao's mother answered for him as she came back in. She passed me a cup of tea, then sat facing us on a sofa. 'My brother has been arrested by the Railway Public Prosecution Organ.'

'Arrested by Public Prosecution? It must be an economic problem,' I said. 'Do you know any details?'

She sighed and said, 'My brother was the general manager of Yunhai Trade Development Company. Their main business was importing and selling household electrical appliances. A large number of such goods now on the market were imported by his company. A few months ago, the head of the Jiangxi Provincial Economic Committee applauded him, saying that his company had not only enlivened the market economy, but also made a great contribution to people's lives. He was held up as a good example. But last Tuesday, the Department of Railway Goods Transport withheld the company's goods and reported him for smuggling to the Railway Public Prosecution Organ. The next day, two people from Public Prosecution went to his office and took him away, and now he's detained in the detention house. It's said that he'll be formally accused of smuggling.' Xiao Zhao's mother could not control herself and her voice choked with sobs. 'Fortunately, you work in the court. You must help me. I know you know the people in Public Prosecution very well. Everything will be dropped if you ask them to let him off. I can give them high rewards.'

The matter was very serious. Apart from the fact that I had only a working relationship with some prosecutors, how could I do as she expected? Even if I had very good friends there, what could I do for her? And yet she looked on me as her hope. I felt overwhelmed by the responsibility.

'Don't be so anxious,' I consoled. 'Let me find out what really happened with your brother first. He will be released if it's nothing serious.'

When Xiao Zhao was seeing me out, he said, 'My grandparents died when my mother was fifteen. My uncle looked after her and supported her till she graduated from university. That's why she's so upset about his arrest. I know this is an awkward matter. I just want you to do your best to help my uncle.'

The following Monday morning, I found time to ring the prosecutor of another case I was handling. When we'd finished talking about that case, I said, 'I heard you've jailed the general manager of Yunhai Trade Development Company. What's his crime?'

'You mean Lei Jiming, that fine example of the individual economy?' he said, full of zest. 'Yes, he'll be charged with smuggling – the chief prosecutor has decided to approve the prosecution. This man is very smart. He's been engaged in smuggling for a while without being caught. But he's fallen into the net of the Railway Bureau since he's been using trains to smuggle the goods. He's gone from being hailed as a good example to being a criminal.'

I didn't question him any further. That the chief prosecutor had decided to approve the prosecution meant that the case was serious and would soon be sent to our court. No doubt Xiao Zhao's mother would say that would make it easier for me to help him. I thought of a friend of mine who had once jokingly asked me whether I would bend the law to help him if he had committed a crime. I answered no, firmly. He asked if I'd do it to help my relatives. I said no again. He laughed and said I was a terrible woman, placing righteousness above loyalty to my relatives and friends. I said I'd have no other choice, but that I believed my relatives and friends would never become criminals in the first place.

This situation was too cruel. I didn't know how I was going to tell Xiao Zhao.

That afternoon, he rang me as I was reading a case file. After I'd told him what I'd heard from the prosecutor, he was cheerful. 'Well, my uncle will be saved when his case is sent to your court, won't he?'

I was so shocked by his comment that I remained tongue-tied for a long time. 'How can you be so sure?' I murmured after he'd hung up the phone.

One month later, as the New Year of 1985 drew near, my colleagues had finished their cases and were preparing to have a relaxing holiday, while I was still busy with an appeal against a death sentence. Of the three days' holiday, I planned to spend only one with Xiao Zhao. As it turned out we only had half a day together, because of an argument. He put a request to me that I couldn't accept.

'Your present job doesn't suit a woman. You cancel our arrangements endlessly. What about after we get married? Will you leave me alone at home like a single man to cook and do the washing by myself? I need my wife to be always at my side. I hope you'll get another job after my uncle's problem has been solved,' he said seriously. 'For me, and for us too.'

I turned and looked into his face. I felt it was so strange to me but I seemed to really understand him then, for the first time. He loved me, I knew that. It was a deep love but also a selfish love. It made me breathe hard. He hoped to have my love all to himself, he was not concerned about my career. He had a traditional Chinese man's view that a woman should only be a good wife and a loving mother. I was sad and disappointed to realise this.

'You wouldn't make such a request if you knew how much hardship I've experienced and how many efforts I have had to make for this job.' I felt a lump in my throat.

Xiao Zhao was disappointed with me too. For a long time we kept silent, not looking at each other. Finally, he broke the silence.

'You know how much I love you. But recently, I often recall you as you were ten years ago, in high school. You were simple then, gentle and lovely. I fell for your singing and your laughing voice, and I was charmed by your dancing. Now you've changed, because of your job. You laugh less and sing less; you're more serious, and calmer. You almost lock yourself up in your work.' He stopped and glanced at me. 'To be honest, I like the former you more. That's why I want you to change your job. Be a teacher, or any light job.'

I cherished his love and I wanted to repay him with mine, but it would be too cruel for me if the price for this was giving up my career. I was a woman, an ordinary woman, and like all women I wanted to love and be loved. I couldn't understand why my career always became a barrier to my love life. I swallowed my words.

Just after the New Year holiday, Chief Judge Liu assigned me another case. 'You young people ought to do more work so that you will improve yourselves quickly,' he justified.

Liu had continued to make things difficult for me where he could – I'd become a thorn in his side. He would assign more cases to me than to other judges, even though they might be free. He always had some sound excuse for doing so, and I couldn't refuse to take a case even if I had a full workload. Furthermore, I didn't want to argue with Liu over his unprincipled behaviour. I locked the case files he'd given me in the filing cabinet and continued with my work.

I hadn't heard from Xiao Zhao for more than a week, and then I had to go to Yingtan for the execution of a rapist. On my return, I felt very dizzy and tired and had to ask for a day's leave. I stayed in bed late, and near lunchtime was woken by a knock on the door. It was Xiao Zhao.

'Are you all right?' He supported me as I returned to my bed, and then sat by me. 'I called your office. Xiao Huang told me you were sick. Do you need to see a doctor?'

'Not really. I just feel a little dizzy. Nothing serious.' I was delighted to see him again.

'You look very tired. You'd better have a few more days' rest,' he persuaded me.

'One day is enough. I have another case to try.'

'Case, case. You always think about your cases.' Xiao Zhao stood up and walked back and forth in the room. 'I'm wondering if there is space for me in your heart.'

'I'm sorry. I'm very appreciative that you've come to see me.'

'I don't want your appreciation, I want your love.' He sat down.

'I do love you. But –'

He covered my mouth with his hand and implored me piteously, 'Don't say but, please.'

'Tell me something about your work.' I changed the topic.

He was in no mood to talk about his work. He stood up, then sat down again. I thought he must have something he wanted to say.

'You said you tried to call me this morning. Is there something you want to tell me?'

'Yes, it's about my uncle.' He looked at me. 'But you're sick. We can talk later.'

I had already guessed what he wanted. He wanted to know if his uncle's case had been sent to my court. And he wanted me to take advantage of my position to help his uncle. I understood that it would be perfect for Xiao Zhao if I helped his uncle to avoid being punished and then gave up my legal career. As payment for these acts, he would give me more of his love. What sort of future would that be for me, I wondered, to get more love by abusing my power and bending the law, and then abandoning my career?

The next day, I went to work as usual. I unlocked the cabinet and took out the case files that Liu had given me over a week before. Something stopped me just as I was about to open the first file. On the hard brown cover, in big black characters, was written 'Crime: smuggling. Defendant's name: Lei Jiming'.

I was stupefied. I stared at the name until it became blurred. I rubbed my eyes, then read it again, character by character. It was him, Xiao Zhao's uncle. Fate had once again played a joke on me, placing me in a sharp dilemma. I faced two choices. One, in accordance with the relevant items of the Criminal Procedure Law, I should withdraw of my own accord and have the case transferred to another judge who was not personally involved. Two, for the sake of Xiao Zhao's love, I could keep quiet, handle the case, and do something for the defendant. The first choice would infuriate Xiao Zhao and his mother, and our relationship would bog down in a crisis. That wasn't my wish; I was afraid of further emotional scarring. But the second choice would go against all my principles as a judge. I would have to leave the court and would no doubt regret it for the rest of my life. This choice made me dizzy and I developed a bad headache.

That night, I went to bed soon after dinner. My parents knew something wasn't right and followed me into my room.

'Ling Ling, is there anything wrong?' my mother asked. 'I don't think it's only your health which makes you eat so little and go to bed so early. Tell us, maybe we can help you.'

I thanked my dear mother and father. They were always at my side whenever I had difficulties. They looked at me with loving eyes, waiting anxiously for my answer. I sat up and nodded my head. My mother draped an overcoat over my shoulders. My father gave me a cup of hot water, saying, 'Don't hurry, drink some first.' I felt like a little girl, though I was nearly twenty-eight.

'I'm sorry. I shouldn't be worrying you any more, I'm an adult now,' I said.

'Don't say that.' My mother smiled. 'In our eyes, no matter how old you are, you're still our little baby.'

I couldn't hold back my tears, not only because of their deep concern but because of my awful predicament. I told my parents the whole story of Xiao Zhao and me.

'Poor girl,' my mother sighed. 'How can you have so much trouble?'

I really regretted sharing my problems with my parents when I saw how worried they were. I forced a smile. 'I feel better now that I've I poured out everything to you. Don't worry about me. I'll work it out by myself.'

My father said, 'I don't want to interfere in things between Xiao Zhao and you, but as far as your work goes, I'd like to say that you'll have no qualms as long as you have a clear conscience.'

My mother sighed again and said, 'Your father and I have been conducting ourselves honestly and uprightly all our lives, and we always hoped our daughters would do the same. Especially now that you're a judge. As you know, I didn't want you to be a judge. I knew it would only bring you difficulties. But since you are a judge now, being upright and incorruptible is your most important duty. I think Xiao Zhao should understand this.'

My parents' advice helped me out of my dilemma and gave me a clear way forward. I felt no hesitation any longer and made up my mind to withdraw from the case. If Xiao Zhao truly loved me, he would understand.

The next morning, the first thing I wanted to do was explain my decision to Xiao Zhao. I thought and thought about how to do this; I knew that for him no explanation would be as good as my agreeing to help his uncle. Suddenly I had an idea. Although I couldn't help his uncle through my own power or connections, I could give him some legal advice on getting a lighter punishment and I could recommend a good lawyer.

From my office I phoned Lao Li, a famous lawyer in Jiangxi province who had more than thirty years of experience.

'I'd be very pleased to take the case and shall do my best,' he said after I had explained the situation. 'But I'd like to say you are too orthodox.'

'Maybe,' I smiled. I then called Xiao Zhao, who was impatient for news.

'Is the case in your court? Who is in charge of it?' he asked before I could say anything. Since he'd asked, I told him the truth. Immediately he began roaring with rage on the phone, almost deafening me.

'If you give up the case, our relationship is finished!' His voice was so loud that I had to take the receiver away from my ear and wait for him to calm down. But he hung up on me. I called him again and again and he repeatedly rang off. I thought he would calm down after a while, and I decided to go and see him that evening.

Next I went to Chief Judge Liu's office to return the case files to him. 'I can't try this case,' I said.

'What did you say? You can't do a little more work? You dare to return it to me? You think you can disregard your leaders?' Liu snapped without waiting to hear my explanation.

'The defendant is my boyfriend's uncle. Do you think I can try it?' I asked when he'd finally stopped.

He saw at once that he'd made a fool of himself and his face turned red. 'Why didn't you say so earlier?'

'You didn't give me time.' I was used to Liu's rough attitude toward me by now.

'Okay, leave them here.' He went on with his reading. I put the files on his desk and left.

As soon as I'd finished work I went to Xiao Zhao's house. His mother half opened the door, then said he didn't want to see me any more. I couldn't believe it and forced my way in. Xiao Zhao was leaning back on a chair with his eyes closed. I called his name and shook his arm. He did not move. I had to turn to his mother.

'Forgive me, Auntie, I had to do this. But I can still help your brother,' I said faithfully. 'I've got a good lawyer for him. Also, I can –'

'Save your fine words now,' she interrupted, 'since you've decided to give up the chance to help him. I don't think you'd be doing so if he was your uncle.'

'Yes, I would. Exactly the same,' I replied.

'I don't know why my son likes you, you have no human feelings whatsoever!' She turned and went into her bedroom. Obviously she had no more interest in talking with me. I glanced at Xiao Zhao. He still sat there without moving. I felt that this family no longer welcomed me and I walked out quietly. The door was shut heavily behind me. I rode my bicycle home, tears streaming down my cheeks.

A few days later, I received a long letter from Xiao Zhao. He scolded me, saying that I didn't understand his love, that I owed him so much yet would not repay him. He said he regretted having loved a woman who wasn't worth it. He ended his letter with: 'I think we should part company. You'd better marry your career.'

It was a stinging attack. My eyes were shedding tears and my heart was bleeding. Once again I had been disappointed in love. I thought Xiao Zhao's last words were right, I'd better marry my career.

不畏压力

UNDER PRESSURE

The breakdown of my relationship with Xiao Zhao caused me to sink into depression. I doubted if there was such a thing as true love in the world. I now understood why in Chinese we do not refer to falling in love, but to talking love – *tan lian ai*. While 'falling in love' has implications of natural feeling, and loving by instinct, 'talking love' has something artificial about it – like talking about business. There will be a marriage if the terms and conditions are satisfactory to both parties. Otherwise, there's no deal.

Failing twice at love made me see that I was not a good talker, and I decided not to talk love with anyone again. I would remain single and focus my whole heart and mind on my career. I tried hard to forget my sadness through work, though it wasn't always easy.

One day, Chief Judge Liu came to assign me a new case as presiding judge – a murder trial. 'This case is special,' he said as he gave me the files. 'The defendant was entitled to exercise legitimate defence, but he exceeded the limits.' He pointed to the defendant's name on the file and warned, 'This man is the nephew of a high-ranked cadre in the municipal Party Committee. You must take that into account.'

Another hard-bone case, I thought wearily – a case of the bone being too hard too bite, too difficult to deal with. I opened the investigation file and began reading. It seemed to be a simple enough matter.

The defendant Fu, aged twenty-nine, was the husband of Chen. Recently Chen had suspected Fu of seeing another woman and often quarrelled with him. On the evening of 23 February 1985 they were quarrelling again in the kitchen when Chen suddenly lunged at Fu with a large kitchen knife, more than twenty centimetres long and nine centimetres wide. Fu's left arm was hurt. When Chen tried to stab at Fu again, he snatched the knife from her and brought the blade down heavily on her skull. She died instantly.

Afterwards, Fu rang the municipal Public Security Bureau to confess his crime. The file also noted that the case had been transferred to the Railway Public Security Bureau as Chen worked in a Railway hospital and both of them lived in accommodation owned by the Railway, but all investigations and tests had been done by the municipal Public Security Bureau.

The record of the inspection of the scene said that Chen had been found lying on the floor in the kitchen. The cut on her head was twelve centimetres long and her skull had been broken. I couldn't go on reading as I felt terribly sick. I turned to another page and saw a photo of the knife and reports on the blood and fingerprints. The blood on the knife and the fingerprints on the handle belonged to both Fu and Chen.

The only witness was a woman called Han, Chen's best friend. Her testimony had been recorded on a cassette. She claimed, 'I saw what happened here. Firstly, Fu and Chen quarrelled, Chen was angry and took the kitchen knife to attack Fu. Then Fu snatched the knife and stabbed Chen. All this happened in a minute.' Fu's own statement was almost the same as the facts confirmed by the Public Security Bureau.

I didn't discover any new information in the prosecution file. The facts were the same as those verified by the Public Security Bureau, and the prosecutor recommended Fu be given eighteen months' imprisonment. The Public Security Bureau agreed. It looked to be a simple case from the existing evidence, but I had an intuition that it wasn't. A woman had been killed, and yet the case had been resolved without further inspection or investigation.

I expressed my doubts to Judge Geng and Judge Shang, the other members of the panel for this case. They had the same uneasy feeling after reading the files.

That afternoon, I received a phone call from a stranger. Without introducing himself he said, 'Don't forget who the defendant Fu's uncle is. Give this clear consideration before judging.' He hung up.

I could not understand how the man had found out I was handling this case so quickly. His meaning was obvious: I should accept the original decision and sentence Fu to no more than eighteen months' imprisonment. I was annoyed: I wasn't going to be forced into doing anything, particularly by someone who was abusing their power.

I was thinking about the case on the way home when a motorcycle suddenly rushed past me from behind, then turned abruptly in front of me, blocking my way. The rider was a young man in a black leather suit and a black helmet.

'Who are you? What do you want?' I knew I didn't know him, though I couldn't see his face clearly in the dark.

'You don't know me but I know you. You're Judge Wang. I also know you're in charge of Fu's case.' The man laughed. 'I want to do nothing but make friends with you. I didn't expect you to be so beautiful.' He tried to touch my face.

'Behave yourself.' I pushed back his hand.

'Don't you think it would be better to be my friend than my enemy?' he said with a ferocious tone.

I looked around. People in the street were all in a hurry. No one had noticed anything was happening here. I felt fear and tried to leave.

'Wait!' He blocked my way again. 'One more thing. You'd better remember that my cousin stabbed Chen to defend himself, it wasn't murder,' he said. Then he rode away quickly.

I took a deep breath and headed home. My mind remained full of the case for the whole night. The young man's words rang in my ears again and again. What did he mean by saying that Fu had acted in self-defence? That it was not murder? So far, no one had said that the defendant was a murderer. Why were these people so anxious to warn me? Perhaps this clumsy denial would result in self-exposure. Was the defendant in fact a murderer? If so, who had stabbed Fu? It would have been impossible for Chen to do so after she had been stabbed herself.

My father in his army uniform, 1950

My mother, Beijing, 1952

My father (third from the left) with his work colleagues, Nanchang, 1953

My mother and my father,
Nanchang, 1954

Me at six months

Back row (L to R): a friend of my father's, two of my cousins, my father. Front row (L to R): Ping, me, Nanchang, 1960

Me aged seven

L to R: Me, Jing, Ping, 1965

L to R: My father, me, Ping, my mother holding Jing, my grandmother, 1965

With classmates at Liantang High School, 1972
(I am on the right in the back row)

With classmates of Nanchang High School, 1974 (I am second from the right)

With my teaching colleagues in Nanchang, 1976 (I am on the right)

With some of my Japanese classmates, Nanchang, 1977 (I am second from the left)

Lao Cai at his home, 1978

First winter at Anhui University, 1979

In the play *Blue Bike*, 1981 (I am on the right)

Me (second from right) with the Anhui University volleyball team, 1981

At graduation, Anhui University, 1982

Outside the Railway Court, 1983

At the Summer Palace, Beijing, 1983

In the courtroom as a court policewoman, 1983

Target practice, 1984

As a presiding judge (second from the right), 1984

In my judge's uniform, 1988

In the study at home, Nanchang, 1988

My father in Shenzhen, 1988

At Beijing University, 1988

With my mother, Nanchang, 1992

L to R: Me, Jing, my mother, Ping, Hui in Nanchang, 1995

How about the witness Han's testimony? The more I thought about the case, the more confused I felt. I decided to check the evidence.

Since I thought Han was very important to the case, I rang her work unit the next morning, only to be told she was sick at home. At lunchtime, Judge Geng and I went to see her at her house. She was in her early thirties and had a childish face.

'You are the only witness to this event,' I said after showing her our work cards. 'We want to know more details about what happened.'

'I . . . I told the policemen on the phone that night,' she whispered.

'That's too simple. We want more details,' said Judge Geng.

Han bent her head. Her whole body was shivering.

Judge Geng and I winked at each other. I went to sit beside Han, saying gently, 'I know that witnessing such an event is horrible. You may feel it's too difficult to recall, or you may have some other concern, but in order to help us find out the facts and give both Chen and Fu a fair judgement, I hope you'll cooperate with us.'

Han remained with her head bent, shivering.

'What time did you go to Chen's home that night?' Judge Geng changed tack.

'About eight o'clock.' Han raised her head.

'What were they doing when you got there?' Judge Geng continued.

Han hesitated.

'Just think about it.'

'They were quarrelling in the bathroom.'

'In the bathroom?' I asked, surprised. Fu had said in his statement that they'd quarrelled in the kitchen.

'Yes.' Han bent her head again. 'Chen was washing a shoe.'

'Since Chen was washing a shoe, how did she get hold of a kitchen knife?' I asked, watching Han closely.

'She . . . she went to the kitchen to get it. No! Chen didn't stab Fu. It was Fu who killed Chen,' Han suddenly shouted, shaking her head and crying. 'Don't ask me any more, please.'

Both Judge Geng and I were shocked at her words. From her behaviour I had a strong feeling that Han was too embarrassed to say what was really on her mind. How were we to judge which testimony was right, this new one or the recorded one?

Returning to the court, I immediately reported the situation to Chief Judge Liu.

'You always look for trouble,' he complained. 'The facts are clearly there in the files. The primary investigation has already been done by the municipal Public Security Bureau. Our Railway Public Security and prosecutor haven't found anything wrong. Why do you like to make cases complicated?'

'I don't want to make the case complicated. It's the case that's not simple,' I argued.

'Well, what's your opinion? Do you believe the witness's new testimony? Do you think the defendant is a murderer? Then tell me who stabbed the defendant. You're not claiming the dead Chen did, are you?' He laughed grimly. 'Don't think you are more talented than anyone else. Don't make trouble out of nothing.'

I left Liu's office feeling, once again, strongly pressured. It was true I did not have enough evidence to prove that Fu had intentionally killed Chen. What should I do next? I was deep in thought.

'Just finish the case as quickly as possible,' Judge Shang advised. 'The chief judge has set the tone, just act upon it.'

'I don't agree,' said Judge Geng. 'The only witness has changed her testimony. We have to reconsider the crime the defendant has committed.'

'But how can you judge which testimony is right? She may change her story again,' argued Judge Shang.

Judge Geng turned to me. 'Since this new evidence has appeared, I think what we should do is ask Public Security to do a further investigation.'

'Liu has already made his attitude clear. I don't think Public Security will accept our opinion,' I said. 'If we aren't afraid of trouble we could do the investigation ourselves.'

'I think you should think about your safety. You're a young woman,' Judge Shang cautioned.

'That's true. Some desperadoes will do anything.' Judge Geng was hesitant.

Our conversation reminded me of the strange men on the phone and on the motorcycle. Maybe I should be more concerned about my own security, but I did not want that to get in the way of making the right judgement. I knew I could apply to withdraw from the case, but I rejected this option because Liu would laugh at me. It seemed I had no other choice but to get to the bottom of it.

The next Monday morning, as I approached the gate of the court, the guard gave me a letter. It was anonymous and read, 'I write to you because I know you are a righteous judge. I hope you won't be frightened of those in power and will punish the killer severely. Fu killed Chen in order to marry another woman. I can't tell you who I am until the defendant has been punished, otherwise I'll be in danger.'

I read the letter repeatedly and then came to a decision: I would start the investigation myself. I made a phone call to Chen's parents, who lived in a small city a hundred kilometres away, and asked them to come to the court. Three days later, Chen's mother arrived.

'My daughter married Fu four years ago,' she told me. 'In the beginning they got along very well, but later they quarrelled a lot. Last October Chen came to see her father and me. I asked her if she and Fu were getting on any better. She cried and said he had another woman and often spent the night with her.'

'Did she say who that woman was?' I interrupted.

'No. She said she saw a photo in Fu's wallet.'

'What photo?'

'A naked woman in my daughter's bed.'

'In your daughter's bed?' I could hardly believe this.

'Yes. Being a doctor, my daughter was often on night shift.' Chen's mother wiped her eyes. 'I don't believe she attacked him first. She still loved him. I tried to persuade her several times to divorce him but she said she couldn't do that. She thought he would change.'

When Chen's mother had left, I set out to discover the

identity of Fu's lover. With two court policemen and a clerk, Xiao Ye, I went to Fu's work unit, a science research institute for the Railway. I learnt from the vice-director that Fu had taken a lot of sick leave recently, but that other workers had reported he wasn't really sick and was seeing a young woman. He had been criticised often for this.

'Do you know who the woman is?' I asked.

'It's said she's a student at Jiangxi University.'

Xiao Ye had brought a search warrant to inspect Fu's personal belongings in the office. The vice-director showed us to Fu's desk, which Public Security had not even touched. In the drawers we found photographs of a naked woman, who looked about twenty, and others of the woman with Fu in bed. Xiao Ye put these in an envelope. We also found dozens of letters sent from Jiangxi University by a woman named Lili, who I thought must be the one in the photos. I was reminded of the words in that anonymous letter: 'Fu killed Chen in order to marry another woman.'

The latest letter had been written four days before Chen died. I skipped the intimate opening and read a paragraph that made my heart beat fast:

> *I wonder how long I still need to wait. You always say, 'Soon, soon, soon,' but you haven't even talked to her yet. You may have forgotten that you said you'd use any method to get rid of her if she didn't agree to a divorce. When will you carry out your promise? I can't wait. I want to be with you every day, not just when she's working. I give you one more week, otherwise I'm leaving you.*

Any method? I wondered. Including killing? Lili had only given Fu one week.

We left Fu's work unit and hurried back to the court. I held a meeting of the panel at once and showed Judge Geng and Judge Shang the photos and letters.

'What do you make of these?' I asked.

'I think they at least prove that Fu had thought of killing Chen during that period,' Judge Geng said after thinking for a while.

'I agree, but we can't say for sure that Fu had the intention of killing Chen that night,' said Judge Shang.

'Of course, not yet.' I was glad we all had the same opinion. 'I plan to go to Jiangxi University to find Lili. She may provide some useful information. I also plan to talk to the witness Han once more.'

Judge Geng and Judge Shang nodded. Just then, a phone call interrupted our discussion. It was Fu's aunt, the wife of the high-level leader. After introducing herself, she said, 'Xiao Wang, I didn't want to bother you but I had to ring you. I heard you haven't yet opened the hearing of my nephew's case because you're doing some investigation. You don't think my nephew killed his wife, do you?' She paused. 'You know his family background. I guarantee he absolutely didn't do that. I know how deeply he loved his wife.'

Hearing her last words, I couldn't help laughing. 'Why are you laughing?' She sounded displeased. 'You laugh at me? Need my husband call you?'

'Oh, no, no.' I didn't want to explain myself to her. 'I shall remember your words. Don't worry, I would never give a wrong judgement to an innocent.'

'Don't play with me! I advise you to think about the consequences if you incorrectly convict my nephew,' she said with an angry voice, then slammed down the phone.

Judge Shang and I laughed, but not Judge Geng.

'I admire your bravery, but I worry about your future,' he said.

'Judge Geng, please don't mention this, otherwise I'll have no courage to go on with it.'

'But you can't avoid thinking about the consequences.'

'It's not that I haven't thought about them, but what good will it bring if all I do is peer ahead and look behind?' I asked. I knew I had to do what was right, even if that meant ending up with the same fortune as my father.

Two days later, I found Lili in her classroom at Jiangxi University. She had a round face, a plump figure, very short hair, and she wore a brown leather jacket. She was the woman in the photos. We had a talk in her room.

'I know you're Fu's girlfriend,' I said straight away.

'No, not any more.' She pointed to a framed photo on her desk by the bed. 'This is my new boyfriend.'

'When did you leave Fu?'

'After he had been detained.' She played with her nails.

'Why? You once loved him very much and wanted to marry him.'

She started. 'How did you know?'

'We know everything,' Xiao Ye interrupted. 'Now we want to see if you are honest or not.'

Lili gave him an unfriendly glance. 'What do you mean? I didn't commit a crime. I didn't ask him to kill his wife, or help him to kill her. I have no involvement in this matter.' She opened a drawer and took out a letter written by Fu. 'This was his last letter before he killed his wife. You'll know I'm innocent after you read it.'

I read it quickly. One sentence mentioned Fu's intention to kill his wife. He wrote, 'Please give me more time. I will talk to her – if she doesn't agree to a divorce, I will take any method to get rid of her, even kill her.' The letter was written on 17 February. Lili's letter, in which she gave Fu one more week, was written on 19 February, two days later, and Chen had died six days after that. I felt the case was getting clearer.

'Then how did you know Fu had killed Chen?' I asked, watching her closely.

She took no heed and just kept playing with her nails. 'That night, he rang me from the detention centre. He said he'd killed his wife for me.'

I stopped her. 'Try to give me his exact words.'

'He said, "Lili, I did it. We can live together very soon." I said, "Has she agreed to a divorce?" He said, in a very low voice, "No, I killed her, you know it's for you." Then he asked me to wait for him. He said he would be released very soon with his uncle's help. I didn't believe it would be that easy. See, I'm right. He is still in jail after nearly three months have passed. How silly I would have been if I had waited for him.'

I stared at this woman, feeling sick. 'So you left him and kept this letter to clear yourself?'

She shrugged her shoulders.

'I really wanted to slap her face,' Xiao Ye said when we'd left her room. 'How stupid to commit a crime like murder for such a woman.'

I could only agree with him. 'Now what we have to do is get more evidence from Han.'

I thought it was also the right time to have a talk with the Public Prosecution Organ. I rang Wei, who was in charge of the case, gave him the new details and suggested he inspect the crime scene and examine the witness again.

Wei was so shocked at my news that he was silent for a few minutes before replying. 'Actually, I had a suspicion that Fu was lying and I wanted to do some further investigation, but I was ordered to issue a bill of prosecution according to the facts confirmed by Public Security. Now, since you've got new evidence, I'll reconsider the case from the beginning.'

'Don't you fear your head will make trouble for you?' I joked.

'Ah! Since you, a fragile lady, are bold and decisive in action, why should I, a manly man, not be?' Wei laughed.

'Good. Xiao Ye will return all the files to you, along with the evidence we have obtained. I shall be waiting for your new bill of prosecution.'

Three weeks later, the prosecutor submitted a new prosecution accusing Fu of murder. After a discussion with Judge Geng and Judge Shang, I decided to open the trial in five days.

It was a cold morning. I got to the court about thirty minutes early but there were already dozens of visitors waiting in the courtroom. A young man with sunglasses ran up to me when I passed by the courtroom to my office.

'We meet again,' he sneered.

'I don't remember meeting you before.'

'But I shall never forget you,' he cursed between his teeth.

I recognised his voice then – he was the man on the motorcycle who had blocked me in the street that day. I raised my voice. 'I know who you are now. I'd like to advise you to stop your foolish behaviour. You'll also be punished if you defy the law.'

Four court policemen nearby hurriedly pulled the man away. He struggled and shouted as he was pushed out of the gate. 'This is an intolerable injustice! I promise you there will be trouble!'

I walked over to him. 'I haven't given any judgement on your cousin so far. The case will be tried in public in ten minutes. You will be allowed to listen if you comply with the rules of the courtroom.'

I took the head of the court policemen aside and urged him to watch the young man carefully. I was worried something bad would happen in the courtroom.

Just before nine o'clock, I entered the courtroom with Xiao Ye and sat in the middle of the cross benches, between Judge Shang and Judge Geng. Fu was brought in and taken to the defendant's box. I looked around the courtroom. The visitors' seats were almost full. Fu's cousin sat in the last row and four court policemen stood close by him.

After checking the defendant's personal details, the prosecutor read the bill of prosecution. Then it was the panel's turn to interrogate the defendant and witnesses.

Under Chinese law, as under Western law, defendants are presumed to be innocent until proven guilty; it is not their responsibility to prove their innocence, but the court's responsibility to prove their guilt. As a judge I was bound to inform the defendant of his rights and advise him that he would be given a just judgement in accordance with the facts.

'According to Item 35 of the Criminal Procedure Law,' I said, 'in cases where there is only the statement of the defendant and no other evidence, the defendant can not be found guilty and sentenced; in cases where there is no statement of the defendant but the evidence is complete and reliable, the defendant may be found guilty and sentenced. It is our government's policy to give leniency to those criminals who confess their crimes and severity to those who refuse to. So I hope you will tell the truth to the court. Do you understand?' I asked the defendant.

'Yes,' Fu replied.

'What was the reason you quarrelled with your wife Chen?'

'Just family things.'

'What family things?'

'She wanted to send more money to her mother. I didn't agree.'

'What were you and Chen doing when you quarrelled?' I asked.

'She was washing dishes in the kitchen and I was standing near her. She raised the knife she was washing to stab me.'

'Do you mean she attacked you first?'

'Yes. When she tried to do it again I got the knife from her and stabbed her.'

'Where did you cut her?'

'I didn't know I had cut her head until she fell down on the floor. Later, I called the police.'

'Show him the knife,' I asked Xiao Ye.

Xiao Ye passed the knife to a court policeman, who took it to the defendant.

'Is that the knife?' I asked Fu.

'Yes,' he admitted after having a look at it.

'Why didn't you get Chen to a hospital?' I stared at him.

'I thought she had died.'

'Was there anyone at your home when this happened?'

'Yes, her friend Han.'

'When did she come and when did she leave?'

'She came before we quarrelled.' Fu raised his head and glanced around the courtroom. 'She left after I called the police. She also told the police what had happened.'

'Do you mean Han saw everything that happened that night?'

'Yes. She confirmed the facts for me that night on the phone.'

'Do you think what you have told us is the whole truth?'

'Yes, of course. The prosecutor is wrong in accusing me of murder.'

I cast Xiao Ye a meaningful glance. 'Bring the witness Han to the courtroom,' he said.

Han looked very frightened when she was led to the witness box.

'Witness Han, please tell the court what you know about the events that happened on 23 February 1985,' said Judge Geng.

'That night, I went to see Chen at her home to say goodbye because the next morning I was going to visit my husband, who serves in the army in Hangzhou. I arrived at her door at about eight o'clock and I heard a quarrel inside. I hesitated, not sure if I should knock or not.

'Then I heard Chen shout, "You want to divorce me to marry that prostitute? No way!"

'Fu's voice said, "Well, it's good you know it. I'll marry her and no one can stop me."

'Chen said, "Don't imagine you can marry her unless you kill me." Then there was quiet. I was about to knock on the door when suddenly I heard Chen shout again, "You really want to kill me. All right, kill me! Kill me!"

'Next I heard Chen give a horrible shriek. I knew something had happened. I knocked on the door anxiously and heavily for minutes. But there was no answer and no sound inside. I kept knocking and shouting until the door opened abruptly. I was dragged in before I saw clearly who it was, and the door was shut and locked immediately behind me. To my left was the bathroom. I saw Chen on the floor, blood covering her face and the floor. There was a shoe in her left hand and a brush by her right hand. I was so frightened I couldn't help screaming and shaking.

'Fu covered my mouth and asked, "Did you hear anything when you were outside?" His eyes made me even more fearful. I couldn't say anything, just shook my head. "Okay, good. Do you know what happened here?" I shook my head again. "Yes, you do know. It was she who stabbed me first, and when she tried to attack me again I had to stab her."

'I couldn't believe what I was hearing and kept shaking my head. Suddenly Fu grabbed my arm tightly, hurting me, and waved a knife before me. "Say what I said!" he ordered me. I had to repeat his words, then he pulled me to the kitchen and made a phone call to someone. I heard him tell his lie and then he said I was the witness. He held the knife to my back and forced me to say what he had told me. I could tell the police on the phone had a close relationship with him, and I had no choice.

'Hanging up the phone, he gave me a strange smile and asked me to take out the medicine box from the cabinet behind the bathroom door. Then he cut his left arm. Blood came out at once and he ordered me to help him wrap it. He said, "Now, you've told the police what happened here. You have to remember that was the truth. You can't change your story, otherwise you'll be punished by law for giving false evidence. I can also say that you're my lover. Now you can go." I left quickly.'

The courtroom was in a tumult. I ordered the visitors to be quiet.

'Defendant Fu, is the witness's account correct?' Judge Geng continued.

'I haven't got another woman to marry. She slandered me,' protested Fu.

Next, Lili was summoned to the courtroom. She told the court everything about the relationship between Fu and herself. Fu denied that he knew Lili until he was shown the photos of them together and his letter to her. Judge Shang then read out the new test report of the scene, which said that some blood spots belonging to Chen were found on the bathroom wall, by the washing-machine and under the basin. Confronted with the evidence, Fu confessed his crime, including details of how he had moved Chen's body to the kitchen after Han had left, to create the impression that Chen had been washing dishes. He declared that he hadn't wanted to kill Chen but had been too angry to control himself.

After closing the interrogation, the prosecutor expressed his opinion and recommended sentencing the defendant to death. Then the lawyer conducted his short defence.

'Please note that my client Fu was a good man. His marriage had broken down, which made him upset. That was why he fell in love with another woman. It was not wrong for Fu to request Chen to terminate a loveless marriage. Chen, by persisting in refusing a divorce, made the matter worse and her words "Kill me" caused Fu to lose control. So I should say Fu had no premeditation in killing Chen, but killed her unintentionally. I ask the presiding judge to consider this point. With regard to his frightening the witness and making her tell a false story, I understand that he was too scared to tell the truth.' Fu's lawyer stopped.

'Is there anything you want to say?' I said to the defendant. 'According to the law, you have the right to make a final statement.'

'I have nothing more to say.'

I declared the trial dismissed.

I held another panel meeting and after discussion we reached a unanimous decision – we judged the defendant guilty of the crime of murder and sentenced him to death.

One week later, the announcement of the judgement was made in public. Fu's cousin attended. Afterwards, he came up to me when I was talking with Chief Judge Liu.

'I didn't know that my cousin had also lied to me. I'm so disappointed with him. I apologise for what I have done to you. Now I understand you and admire your uprightness and courage. I really want to be friends with you. Believe in my good faith, please,' he said with a friendly smile.

'Very good! Xiao Wang is very nice and she is still single.' Liu gave me a sideways glance.

I knew he was deriding me but I didn't want to contradict him. I was in a good mood as I hadn't worked in vain and the case had been finished successfully at last.

'Thank you. I have to go to work now. Bye,' I said politely to the young man, and walked away.

单身烦恼

THE VEXATION OF BEING SINGLE

One thing Chief Judge Liu said was right. I was still single, though I was nearly twenty-eight. The legally prescribed marriage age in China at that time was twenty for women and twenty-two for men, and the preferred ages were twenty-three and twenty-five respectively. People who hadn't married by the preferred age were called old youth. There was no doubt about it, I had become one of them automatically.

According to traditional Chinese custom, a woman was thought to have some kind of problem if she hadn't married by the age of twenty-five, especially if she was good-looking, had a good family background or a secure professional job. People liked to gossip about such women behind their backs. Some parents even felt ashamed of their daughters if they didn't have husbands by the right age. This pressure from society and family caused many women to regard marriage as their duty, and to choose it in a slapdash manner.

A friend of mine, Jiang Yan, had been busy with her study and didn't fall in love with anyone until she met Ge, a divorced man, at twenty-seven. Unfortunately, Ge's mother objected. She thought there must be something wrong with Jiang Yan, otherwise such a highly educated and pretty woman would have married much earlier. So she did some investigations and came to the conclusion that Jiang Yan was infertile. In order to put a stop to their relationship, Ge's mother went to Jiang Yan's work unit, censuring her in public. Jiang Yan couldn't bear such slander and shame. She left Ge and married a man she didn't love two months later, and in order to prove herself fertile she had a son a year after that.

I didn't want to drift into the same rut, although I knew there had been some talking behind my back since I'd parted from Zhao. Some people said the conditions I set were too high. Some thought I might have been provoked by a previous love. Since I did not want to have to defend myself, I pretended to have heard nothing, reassuring myself that I could take the way that I wanted and let others say what they wanted. But some warmhearted people showed their concern about my lack of a husband.

One day in September 1985, I got to the office early. Judge Geng came to see me with a case file, saying, 'Chief Judge Liu told me that you're to be the presiding judge on this case; Judge Zheng and I are to be the other members of the panel. I've read this file. Please pass it on to Judge Zheng once you've finished with it.'

I glanced at the file and smiled bitterly. Another rape case. I knew Liu was making things difficult for me. All the cases he assigned me were either problematic or related to sex. I felt that he should have been considerate of the fact that I was the only single female judge in the court, and given such cases to other judges. In some cases I had had to read very detailed accounts of how the accused had raped his victims, often several pages worth of description that read more like a pornographic novel than a legal file. I tried to skip over them as much as possible as I was embarrassed to read such things, but sometimes I had to read carefully in order to get at the facts.

'I know this case isn't suitable for you.' Judge Zheng was sympathetic when I gave him the file. 'But it would be easier if you were married. I think you should give this matter active attention, since you're not young any more.'

'Actually, I want to stay single all my life,' I told him.

'That's not practical. Everyone must get married eventually.'

'I disagree that marriage is a task that everyone must accomplish,' I argued.

'You'll feel lonely when you're old. You can't imagine at the moment what a miserable and dreary life it will be alone.' Judge Zheng looked as if he had deep feelings on the matter. 'It's said couples are lovers when they are young and companions when they are old.'

When it came to love, I believed in predestination. 'What you said sounds quite reasonable,' I replied, 'but I think the most important elements for two people getting married are understanding each other well and loving each other deeply, and this understanding and love can't be pursued, but only found by chance.'

'I agree with Xiao Wang.' Judge Geng came in and joined

our conversation. 'Be honest, it's really difficult for Xiao Wang to find a suitable husband.'

'I don't agree.' Judge Zheng was adamant that I was an eligible candidate for a future husband. 'Xiao Wang is beautiful, talented and sensible; she has a good job and a good family background. With such fantastic prerequisites, how can it be difficult for her to find a suitable husband?'

'The difficulties come from those very same fine attributes. According to traditional custom, she must marry a man with better prospects than she has. But as her own are so good, where can she find a man whose are better?' Judge Geng gave me a glance and continued. 'Now, girls who have no diploma also want to marry a young man with a high degree. Xiao Wang has a Bachelor of Arts degree, so her husband must have one at least the same level.'

'Yes,' Judge Zheng agreed.

'Well, a great number of people are already excluded.'

'I suppose so.' Judge Zheng nodded.

'Xiao Wang's husband must also be handsome and taller than she is. That means he must be 1.8 metres or so.'

'Another large number of people will be excluded,' Judge Zheng smiled.

'Right. Xiao Wang is nearly twenty-eight. Her husband must be older than that. Also, he must be smart and have a good job and a bright future. By now there are very few eligible people. According to Xiao Wang's belief, they must understand each other and love each other.' Judge Geng shook his head. 'So it's as difficult as fishing for the moon.'

'I don't think so.' It was Lin, the president of the court, who had come in quietly, a cigarette between two fingers. 'You're talking about Xiao Wang's great event for life, aren't you?'

'Yes. What's your brilliant idea?' asked Judge Zheng.

'Why must her husband have better prospects than she does? Sometimes we should be flexible. For example, Xiao Hu, the younger son of the director of the political department of the Railway Bureau, is a good choice,' Lin suggested.

'I know him.' Tu Ke, who had been reading, interrupted. 'He is a friend of my younger brother. The president is right. Maybe it's good for Xiao Wang to marry a man of a little lower condition, like Hu.'

'Why?' Judge Geng asked.

'If the man's conditions are very low, the couple would have no common language. If the man's conditions are higher, he would hope only for her to be a good wife, but Xiao Wang has a strong career mind – she will not be willing to give up her own career just to look after her husband. So Hu is the right person. He has no higher ambitions but has a good job. In other aspects they are well matched. He will also take on all the housework in order to support Xiao Wang. I know he is a good cook.'

'Xiao Wang needs a husband, not a housekeeper,' Judge Geng objected.

I listened to their animated discussion quietly. About one hour had passed but they had no intention of finishing. It seemed unlikely they'd reach a decision soon. I couldn't help laughing in my sleeve. Since I knew they were doing this out of kindness, I didn't want to stop them; I took some files and sneaked off.

When I came back to the office some time later, Tu Ke approached me. 'Where have you been? I suggest you give Hu careful consideration on the weekend. Don't laugh, I'm serious. Give me an answer on Monday, then I can build a bridge for you two.'

'Let me off, please.' I pleaded. 'I have enough vexation on weekends.'

Thinking of weekends gave me a headache, as I had to listen to my mother's interminable chatter on exactly the same topic. She had said to me repeatedly by now, 'You're nearly thirty, you can't live with your parents forever. A person has two important things to do in life, set up a family and embark on a career. You can't put all your heart and mind into your career.' At first I tried to stop her worrying by promising to meet new men. As a result I was often asked to meet someone on Sundays, but since I had decided not to talk love any more, I always found an excuse to leave early.

My mother saw through me quickly and scolded me for lacking sincerity. 'Since you agree to meet them, you should give them serious consideration. Your present attitude is not polite.'

After that, I wouldn't agree to meet anyone. Every Sunday morning I left home early, spending all day in the city library, until it closed. My mother was upset. She thought she could do nothing for me, so my father had to become involved.

One Friday evening, I was reading a book in the study while my sisters slept. Jing was now working in the Bank of China in Nanchang. Despite being sent to the countryside, she'd later managed to enter university and study accountancy. My elder sister Ping had married the year I graduated from university and was still living in Nanchang. She too had gone to university and was now the Manager of Jiangxi Packaging Company. My youngest sister Hui was studying at high school.

My father called me gently. 'Ling Ling, come out! I have something to say to you.' From his serious expression I sensed what he wanted to talk to me about.

I put down my book, went to the living room and sat on the long sofa, near the one on which my father was sitting. I looked at his face, waiting for his lecture. He didn't look at me but said slowly in a low voice, 'You may have guessed what I am going to say. As is normal, your mother has given much thought to your marriage, and as a father I needn't interfere. But your attitude has made your mother very anxious and she often suffers from insomnia.' He turned his eyes to me. 'This is the first time, and also the last time, that I'll give you my opinion. It's up to you if you accept it or not. I know you'll make your own judgement and won't be influenced by others. Actually, your mother and I don't want to force you to do anything. All we do is for your good. We are getting old. One day we'll leave you, and then who will take care of you when you are in need? I understand how your failing in love twice has grieved you deeply, but you should let time heal your wounds and let new love help you forget your pain. You are a woman of strong character, you have overcome one difficulty after another and experienced many setbacks. How can you admit defeat on this matter? Fragrant grass can be found everywhere. Forget the past, seek true love, and set up a happy family – these are your mother's desires and also mine.'

I lowered my head, my tears out of control. I was deeply moved by my parents' affection and understanding, and I felt guilty for having caused them disappointment and worry. But I felt distressed, too, at the thought that love had passed me by. I also felt embarrassed, for I didn't know if I should accept my father's advice.

'I hope you'll think over my words carefully.' My father passed me a photo of a young man. 'This is Xinyu. His mother is a friend of your mother's. Although his appearance is mediocre and he's only 1.74 metres in height, he's a nice man, honest, reliable, and he has great prospects. He's doing a PhD in America at present. He's heard a lot about you from his mother and is well disposed toward you. You can write to each other first if you like. We don't mean you must marry him, but do give serious consideration to it.'

My father stood up. 'All right, it's rather late. I won't say any more.' He walked to his bedroom.

Gazing at his grizzled hair and thin figure, I felt I was really selfish. I never thought about my parents' feelings, only my own.

I was torn by conflicting thoughts for many days, and often sat in the office with case files before me but reading nothing. My determination to remain single was starting to shake. I tried to persuade myself that I should give it up, at least for my parents. I also recalled the trouble I had had because of being single. While most staff got an extra allowance, I didn't because I had no family responsibilities. And while most staff enjoyed their festival holidays and only a few were asked to be on duty, I was always asked because I had no children to look after.

Being unmarried had also caused me some embarrassment. Not long before, a single clerk at the court had been having illicit relations with a married woman. The woman's husband found out and asked the organisation to help. The young man was not only ordered to submit a written statement of repentance, but was also criticised in a document that was read by every member of the court staff. However, the document did not mention the man's name, but said, 'A highly educated single staff member not concerned with other's family happiness has had illicit relations with another's spouse.' Apart from that young man, I was the only single, highly educated staff member in the court. People who didn't know me well couldn't help wondering whether it was him or me. I imagined people carrying on endless discussions about this, and although such a misunderstanding was harmful to my reputation, I couldn't explain to everyone to clarify the facts. I only repeated to my heart, I'm innocent. I finally felt free when the young man committed the mistake again and the husband came to the court, exposing everything in public.

One morning, while I sat in my office lost in thought, I got a phone call from Director Dong of the Railway Bureau's Women's Federation, which was in charge of women's affairs. All matters relating to women, such as their education and training, family issues, entertainment, welfare, and, most importantly, permission to have a child, were taken care of by the Women's Federation. This was the second time Dong had called me and I knew what she wanted before she spoke.

As I'd suspected, she was calling to ask if I needed permission to have a child. Because the Chinese population was already so large, the government had placed restrictions on the number of children a couple could have – in most cases this was one child per couple – and any woman who wanted to have a child had to get permission from the relevant authority in her work unit. There was a quota for the number of permissions that could be granted each year, and older women had priority. This meant that some younger couples might have to wait for a few years before they could have a child. The irony was that women like me could be part of the quota even when they didn't need to be. Dong knew well that I hadn't married yet, but she still did her routine duty as director of the Women's Federation.

'Don't ask me this question again, please,' I told her. 'I will let you know when I need it.'

'All right, all right.' Dong laughed down the phone. 'But I have another thing to tell you. The Party Committee of the bureau has decided to establish a committee for protecting women's legitimate rights and interests.'

'That's good,' I said.

'Yes, and I was asked to inform you that the Party Committee, after discussions with the president of your court, has appointed you the chairperson. You have knowledge of the law and are qualified for this work.'

'But I am busy with my judicial work.' I felt the role was not right for me but I couldn't clearly say why.

'The committee has five other members. They will solve all the small problems,' Dong explained.

Since it had been decided, and I need only deal with the big matters, I accepted.

One hour later, I received the appointment certificate. It made my colleagues laugh.

'It's really interesting,' Xiao Huang said. 'I don't know how they even considered it. This job should have been given to an older married woman, such as Tu Ke.'

'Yes, Xiao Huang is right,' said Judge Zheng. You can't accept this job. You'll be dealing with family matters almost every day and you'll be fed up with them.'

'What can I do? It was the leaders' decision. Anyway, I only need to become involved with the major problems.' I was reassuring myself as much as them.

As it turned out, work on the committee started the next morning. I received more than ten calls on the first day, mostly from women, and almost all of them complained about their husbands. I had to put my other cases aside at times. At first I told the women I was busy and that there were full-time members in charge of these matters, but they insisted on talking to me, saying they trusted only me because I was a legal person. I found it difficult to refuse to help them. I spent many hours a day receiving all kinds of women and giving them legal advice.

Before long I felt deeply that this role was not suitable for a single woman like me. Giving legal advice was not hard, the difficulty was listening to their private stories, which always made me shy and on which I was unable to give an opinion.

Late one afternoon, I was on my way to a meeting when an old woman and a young woman knocked on the door. They requested to see me immediately. Xiao Huang, who sat beside the door, asked them to wait, but the old woman began talking at once. I conducted the two women to a small meeting room and said, 'You are so anxious to see me. Tell me quickly how I can help you.' I was a little impatient as my normal work had been interrupted.

'Save my daughter, please, she can't go back to her home!' the old woman cried. 'She can't live with that awful man any longer. Look at her, she barely looks human in appearance now because she has been subjected to his torments. She is only twenty-six but looks nearly forty.'

The young woman sat there silently. She looked pale, downcast and a little shy. I didn't know what had happened but I already sympathised with her.

'Can you tell me what happened to you? Maybe I can help,' I said gently.

The young woman at once started sobbing and told me her story in a tearful voice. 'I'm Juanjuan. One year ago, I married Fan, who was introduced to me by a colleague of mine. As soon as we married I got to know he –' She suddenly stopped.

'Go on, please.'

'He wants . . .' Her face reddened.

'Don't be shy and just tell Judge Wang,' her mother encouraged.

The daughter glanced at her mother and then at me and said, 'He wants too much sex.'

Hearing the word 'sex', I felt uneasy from head to foot. 'Don't tell me everything, just let me know why your mother said you have been suffering from your husband.'

'It's just sex.'

I started at her repeating that word. I had to ask her to explain it to me. She stared at me. 'Can I go on?'

'Yes.'

'My husband wanted to make love with me at least once a night. But twice was very common. Sometimes he asked me to go home from work. In the beginning, I felt I couldn't refuse him, though I was always too tired. He also said he wanted me because he loved me. How could I refuse his love? But after a few months, I felt dizzy and exhausted. I often fell asleep in the office. My leader criticised me for not working well and my colleagues laughed at me, saying that I had too much sex. I felt ashamed and was scared when night came. And at work I was afraid of hearing someone say my husband was calling me.

'One evening after dinner, I told him my thoughts and hoped he would understand. But without letting me finish, he pulled me to the bed rudely, saying, 'I want you right now.' I was so disappointed that I lay in bed, eyes brimming with tears, and let him do what he wanted. After getting satisfaction, he got off my body, hummed a tune and left the room. He didn't even glance at me. I suddenly had a feeling which I had never had before – I started to feel disgust for him and thereafter hated to make love with him.'

Juanjuan was too upset to keep speaking. I gave her a cup of tea and tried to calm her down. She took a deep breath and told me that, since then, the frequent sex had changed to violence. As long as she refused him, she would be beaten. After a while, she could no longer bear such mental and physical suffering and went back to live with her mother. She still hoped her husband would change his behaviour. In fact, her husband didn't want to be a good husband at all. He went to her mother's home to beat her and forced her to go back.

'I have no affection for him at all now. He didn't love me, he just wanted to torment me. What I want is to leave him. But he said it's impossible. I can't divorce him as long as he disagrees, and he would never agree to a divorce. Furthermore, he said he had a right to have sex with me whenever he wanted because he was my husband. I don't know if what he said is right. If it is, I would rather die.' She showed me the bruises on her body.

'If what you say is true, then according to the marriage law and the criminal law, you can not only apply for and get a divorce from him, but you also can sue him for rape if he dares to try to force you to make love again.' I stood up. 'I have much work to do. You can contact me if you have any problems.'

'You mean I can apply for a divorce now?' The young woman seemed not to dare to believe what I'd told her.

'Yes, if you want. But I suggest you consider it carefully before you take any action. Marriage and divorce are big issues in a person's life.'

Seeing off the two women, I went into deep thought. Since I had been doing this extra work, I had received dozens of complaints from women. Most of the problems were to do with their marriages. By the 1980s the rate of divorce in China was very low, but the quality of many marriages was also low, the major reason being that most women born in the early 1960s and before had still been affected by traditional Chinese thought. There was a saying that 'a good woman won't marry twice'. Thinking of this, I grew more determined to remain single.

Back home that evening, I spoke to my father during dinner. 'Father, I have been thinking of your words these past days, but I'm afraid I can't set up a closer relationship with Xinyu. Also, I don't want to treat marriage as a task to be completed, but I promise you I'll bring you a son-in-law if one day I meet a person I can't leave.'

My father nodded. 'All right. We don't want to force you to do anything. I hope I will see that day when you bring an excellent young man home.'

I didn't dare say, 'You will,' because by then, in my heart, I was uncertain whether that day would ever come.

In China in the 1980s social dances were popular in almost all cities. Most were held by work units and featured Western dances such as the tango, waltz, cha-cha, and so on. I had learnt this kind of dancing at university and often went to dances held by the court. But whereas students and other young people danced for the pleasure of it, many of those who went to dances held by work units were looking for future partners. In those years, many couples had their first encounter during a dance.

I met a lot of people who were on the look-out in this way. As soon as the music started they began their questions. Whatever name you told them, they would say it was beautiful, or 'as pretty as yourself'. Then they would ask your age, and if you told them they would say you looked much younger than that.

Normally I refused to answer this question, but asked them to guess. Of course they always said a younger age on purpose. The next question would be occupation. Again I let them guess. It was interesting that no one could ever guess right. They thought I was a doctor, teacher, artist or an actress. They didn't believe I was a judge, even after I told them.

There was one question they didn't ask, which was whether you were married or not, as this was assumed. Thinking you were single, they wouldn't let you off. They would invite you to a dance somewhere else. I didn't object to others looking for their future spouses at dances, but I was not willing to do so. So I always refused the invitations, no matter who they were from and what they were for.

On 8 March, International Women's Day, all working women had half a day's holiday. We usually attended a very short celebratory meeting and then saw a film. Actually, nearly half the cinema audience was often men. Many married women gave their tickets to their husbands and stayed at home to do housework.

On International Women's Day in 1986 I saw Director Dong at the cinema. She gave me an invitation to a party the Women's Federation was holding that night. 'We have arranged that you'll give a speech, to encourage the women, give them legal advice, and tell them how to protect themselves.' When she saw that I was keeping silent, she warned, 'Don't refuse. They need your help.'

I went to the party on time. Hundreds of people were already in the big hall. To my surprise, there were not only women but also many men there. After announcing the start of the party, Dong introduced me to everyone. 'I'm pleased to welcome the chairwoman of our Committee for Protecting Women's Legitimate Rights and Interests, Judge Wang Ling, to our party. Judge Wang has devoted all her love and energy to her work, so she has had no time to concern herself with personal matters. Now, let's invite her with welcoming applause to give us a speech.'

Dong's introduction caused me much trouble. My speech was followed by a dance and I quickly became the target of many men. I danced almost from the beginning to the end as I was invited continuously.

The next day, I received a phone call from Dong. She said she had something urgent to discuss with me. We met in her office one hour later.

'You must thank me as I've done you a big favour,' she smiled.

I was puzzled and didn't understand.

'Silly girl. Someone has taken a fancy to you. It's the only son of the minister of the Provincial Personnel Department. The family background is no doubt excellent. He is a photographer, tall and handsome. Many girls are pursuing him but he has not settled on anyone. He said he fell in love with you at first sight. Do you remember, he invited you to dance twice?' Dong looked excited. 'I didn't expect my introduction to have such good results. I know you're finding it hard to get a suitable man. Take my advice and don't miss this chance. It's not easy to find a man who doesn't mind that you have a higher degree and a higher position than he has. He asked me to pass on his message.'

I looked at and listened to her with a smile. I understood why she had introduced me the way she had and I appreciated her kindness in my heart, but at the same time her help left me not knowing whether to laugh or cry.

'He doesn't dislike my higher degree and position but I dislike his lower degree,' I said, making fun. 'Director Dong, I really appreciate your help, but I have limited time and you know my judicial work is very busy. If I agree to talk love with him, can you select another chairwoman of the committee?'

'No, no. They're two separate things,' Dong answered hurriedly.

'Well, forget about giving such help then, please. I have no time to concern myself with personal things at the moment.'

My answer disappointed her, I could see. In fact, it was not only Dong – I made many people disappointed and even annoyed. Within one week I received more than a dozen letters from young men who had met me that night. I didn't open even one of them, although I knew it was not polite or fair to the men and that they would berate me behind my back. In order to avoid such distressing consequences, I seldom went to dances or parties after that.

是赢是输
Win or Lose

By 1986 *Yanda* was in its third and final stage. I can't recall just how many cases I handled, and how many had gone smoothly, with no conflict, but it seemed to me that even the smallest of cases was not easy to handle. The great majority were for hooliganism, and one such involved an appeal. The defendants were four teenagers, aged between sixteen and eighteen. The original judgement had sentenced them to a fixed-term imprisonment of from three to four years. The first defendant, Chang, had submitted an appeal petition.

The files were quite thick and disorganised. I spent a few days coming to grips with the case, and I noticed five key points. One, the case had occurred two years ago, three months before *Yanda* started. The four defendants had received criminal detention for one month for engaging in hooligan activities (in this case, jointly having sex with a woman). Two, when *Yanda* began, the four defendants were arrested again. The Public Security Bureau recommended prosecuting the defendants for jointly committing rape in succession, because the woman they had had sex with had accused them of it. Three, in spite of the woman's statement, the four defendants denied having raped the woman, and there was no other evidence to prove it. Four, the woman was over thirty years old and had already been detained for prostitution several times before now. Five, the prosecutor thought the evidence was not sufficient to prove the crime of rape and returned the case to Public Security for more evidence. Public Security sent the case back again without supplying more evidence – over the course of a year, the files were sent back and forth between the two organisations. At last an agreement was reached that saw the defendants prosecuted for hooliganism.

After checking the four defendants' statements and the testimony of a witness, Datou, Chang's neighbour, I thought the evidence was conclusive and the facts could be confirmed as follows: on the evening of 5 July 1983 the four defendants were walking along the street when a woman came up to ask them if they could find a place for her to sleep. The first defendant, Chang, gave the others a meaningful glance and answered, 'You want to find a place to sleep? No problem. Just follow us. We'll take you to a place without charge.'

Chang walked ahead with the other defendants and the woman followed them. The second defendant asked Chang, 'What do you mean?'

'This woman must be a prostitute. We'll take her to Datou's house to play with her.'

Soon they arrived at Datou's house, which was actually a small restaurant. Chang asked the others to wait outside and went in by himself. After a few minutes he came out with Datou, a boy of seventeen. Chang said to the woman, 'This is my friend.

His parents run this restaurant but they are not at home. There's a big storeroom upstairs with a lot of empty space. You can live there for free.'

The woman smiled at Datou, saying, 'Thank you.' Then she turned to Chang. 'Can you come upstairs with me?'

Datou walked first and Chang second, then the woman, followed by the three other defendants.

'You can put the tables together.' Datou pointed to two square tables and said to Chang, 'I have to go downstairs. Call me if you need anything.'

As soon as Datou left, Chang asked the other defendants to move the tables together. The woman jumped on them and lay down. She asked the defendants to sit on the table around her. After a few minutes of talking, the woman said she was hot and took off all her clothes. The four defendants stayed still, looking at each other. The woman then asked Chang to take off his clothes and get on her body.

Chang did as the woman instructed. Afterwards, the woman asked Chang, 'Do you have any money?'

'Yes, I'll pay you,' said Chang.

On the instruction of the woman, the three other defendants had sex with her in turn. Later, Chang called Datou to send in some toilet paper. The woman asked Datou to have sex with her. Datou said he didn't know how to do it. The woman told him it didn't matter, she had taught the other four boys and could also teach him. Datou was too scared to accept her offer and asked them to leave.

The four defendants gathered seventy-two yuan to give

the woman and told her to find another place. The woman was not happy with the amount and cursed them loudly as she left the house.

I thought that, in view of the facts, the circumstances were minor and could not be deemed to be a crime. And given that the four defendants were first offenders and had already been detained for one month, they shouldn't be prosecuted twice for the same offence. If they had been arrested again because the woman had accused them of rape, they should be released since the rape could not be verified. I couldn't understand why the court in the first trial had judged them hooligans, and why such a small case had lasted so long a time. Adopting a prudent policy, I went to see the judge of the first trial instead of just revising the original judgement.

Unfortunately I didn't get any useful information from the original judge. All he told me was that the court's judicial committee had made this judgement. He suggested I talk to the policeman and prosecutor who had handled the case, because the heads of the Public Security Bureau and the Public Prosecution Organ had been involved in the judgement.

I met the prosecutor in his office. He was not much older than I, and looked kind and honest. I shared my questions and opinions. He said with a smile, 'When I heard you were hearing this case, I knew you would submit a different opinion on the judgement. As I expected, you have come asking about it.'

'It sounds as if you have recognised something wrong with the judgement.' I smiled. 'Can you tell me your own opinion?'

'I'll tell you honestly that I hold the same view as you. But I'd also like to advise you not to be too sharp. We are only ordinary legal people; we can't expect to change our heads' minds, but must obey their orders, as a soldier obeys his commanding officer.' He sighed with deep feeling. 'I was transferred here from the army two years ago and I've found it's been more difficult dealing with the complicated interpersonal relationships than dealing with the cases.'

I was surprised to learn from the prosecutor that the first defendant's father was working in Public Security. He was a dauntless man with nearly forty years' experience, and because of his character there wasn't a leader who didn't hate him. They hadn't found a chance to vent their spite until his son's case, but it was obvious that this was the reason why the case had lasted two years, and why they had decided to prosecute the defendants as hooligans when they were unable to confirm the crime of rape.

Now that the case had been appealed and had come to my court for the second trial, these leaders couldn't extend their influence, I realised. I reported the details of the case to the judicial committee of my court. It was not a small matter to revise the original judgement and render the defendants a judgement of not guilty – it meant denying all the work done by Public Security and the Public Prosecution Organ. It also meant that the defendants would be released immediately.

After more than four hours of discussion, the judicial committee could not reach a final decision because one member was absent and the rest voted three to three, holding two opposite opinions.

I learnt after the meeting that the head of Public Security and the chief prosecutor of the intermediate court – not the same people who'd been involved in the initial trial – had held their own meeting beforehand. They'd decided to confirm the original judgement because they thought that work morale in Public Security would be damaged if the defendants were released. The president of my court, and Judge Liu of course, wanted to support them, but unfortunately they couldn't win a majority on the judicial committee. So the case was referred to the political-legal committee, a temporary institution which had been set up during *Yanda* to reconcile any disagreements between *Gong, Jian, Fa* (the Public Security Bureau, the Public Prosecution Organ and the courts). The committee consisted of the three presidents of *Gong, Jian, Fa*.

I had no idea what to expect as I walked into the meeting. I looked quickly at everyone sitting around the long table, feeling some eyes looking at me with displeasure. I thought it boded ill rather than well. I took a chair near the door, keeping a little distance from them. Suddenly I heard my name called. It was a man in his late fifties, big and tall with a kindly smile.

'Xiao Wang, come sit here.' He pointed at the chair next to him. I smiled and got up to sit beside him.

'It's the first time that we meet, although I have heard your name many times.' He extended his hand. 'I'm Sun Huoda, the director of the committee.'

I shook hands with him, glancing at those people who were watching us with dissatisfied expressions.

'Now, we will start our meeting. Who has read all the files

of this case?' Director Sun looked at the three chiefs one after another, waiting for their answer.

'I haven't read them but I've heard the report of the panel,' said President Lin.

'I haven't had time to read all the files,' said the chief policeman.

'How about you, Chief Prosecutor?' Director Sun asked when he saw him keeping silent.

'I haven't read them but I know the details of the case.'

'Okay, I know you're too busy to read all the files. It doesn't matter as Xiao Wang is here. As you know, she is the presiding judge of the case and can give you a detailed introduction.' Sun winked at me.

I spent nearly one hour introducing and analysing the case. Finally, I said, 'According to the facts and the law, I, as well as the panel, think we should judge the defendants not guilty and release them immediately.'

'What do you think of Xiao Wang and her panel's opinion?' asked Sun.

There was a long silence. Sun put his question again. Then the chief prosecutor opened his mouth.

'I have heard different reports about the defendants' criminal behaviour, which is more serious than Xiao Wang has told. I think we should make sure of the facts first.' He looked at the chief policeman. 'Isn't that right?'

President Lin didn't say anything, but kept smoking. Sun grew impatient. He put the files in the middle of the table. 'We have no time to sit here still talking about the facts. Since 1983, this case has been transferred from Public Security to Public Prosecution, then to the courts. More than two years have passed and you haven't even read the files. I understand you have a lot of work to do, but how can we confirm the facts of a case just by relying on reports? If we don't read the files for ourselves, how can we know if the reports are correct or not?' He stopped for a moment. 'I have spent one and a half days reading all these files. So I know the details and I can say surely that Xiao Wang's report on the case is correct. I completely agree with her opinion.'

Everyone was greatly surprised at these words but no one said anything. Director Sun continued, 'If you have doubts about the facts, I suggest you take the files back to have a careful reading. But for the moment, I want you to express your opinion about the judgement on the basis of the facts which the presiding judge has confirmed.'

Another long silence followed. I glanced at my watch — we'd been there for more than two hours. I was getting uneasy since I had much work to do.

'Can I leave now?' I asked Director Sun in a low voice. 'I've got another case in hand.'

'Yes, you will be informed of the final decision later.'

Back in my office, I didn't give any more thought to the case or the meeting, or to what would happen to me, but started on a new case.

Lao Liang, who was responsible for taking down the notes of the meeting, told me later that the meeting had lasted all day and the argument was heated. Finally, but reluctantly, the three heads agreed with Director Sun's opinion.

'You have won the case, but be careful! I could feel that the three heads were very displeased, especially President Lin, because he had lost to you again,' Lao Liang told me.

How could I be careful? It seemed to be my fate not to avoid difficulties. A few months before, Chief Judge Liu had wanted me to move to another division, citing the excuse of my safety, as I was the only woman judge in the criminal division. Jiao, the Party Secretary of the court, objected after he heard of my willingness to remain, but I thought it would be really hard to continue working as a criminal judge this time, since I had annoyed all three heads of *Gong, Jian, Fa*.

Late that afternoon, I had packed up the things on my desk and was about to go home when President Lin came to my office, quietly, without any expression on his face. He informed me of the final decision and asked me to finish the other cases I was handling as soon as possible.

From that time on, I was given no new cases and I knew my hunch was right. Soon after, there was a rumour in the court that I was going to leave the criminal division because I considered its leaders beneath me.

One month later, in the middle of April, President Lin announced a couple of appointments at a meeting of all the court staff. One of them was me as the deputy-chief judge of the commercial division. This was beyond anyone's expectation, including mine, and everybody began talking about it.

'As I said before, leaders are heavyweight and we are lightweight. It's impossible for the lightweight to beat the heavyweight. See, my words have been proven right,' said Judge Shang.

'What you said is half right and half wrong,' argued Judge Geng. 'The lightweight has little chance to win over the heavyweight, but I don't think Xiao Wang has lost, she's won.'

'I don't think she's won or lost,' Judge Zheng insisted. 'She's been transferred from the criminal division but been promoted at the same time. So the conflict between her and the three heads has ended in a draw.'

'I agree with Judge Geng.' Xiao Huang, who was binding files, joined in. 'If Xiao Wang has been promoted and transferred at the same time, then she's the winner.'

'Everybody stop, please!' I shouted, smiling. 'Don't argue about this any more. No matter whether I've won or lost, I have to say goodbye to all of you.' I felt a little sad just saying so. 'But I'm lucky I haven't been transferred out of the court altogether, and am only changing offices. We can still see each other every day.'

'Don't be upset. Anyhow, you're a leader now. It's a symbol of your success,' Judge Geng confirmed.

'I hope you'll always be the present you,' said Xiao Huang.

'I will. I won't change my principles as a human being,' I promised him, and myself as well.

That evening, when I told my parents what had happened, they were very pleased. Besides the fact that I'd been promoted, they were happy to hear I had left the criminal division.

'Now I can stop worrying about your safety.' My mother breathed deeply. 'You don't know how anxious I was, waiting for your return when you went away investigating a crime.'

'But trying criminal cases is the most important work in

the court. In the commercial division I'll only be handling commercial disputes, and there aren't many of them at the moment.' I couldn't help expressing my disappointment to my parents.

As usual, my father brought me round. 'You may have noticed that the economy has developed quickly in these past years. Economic disputes will increase year by year, and solving these by means of the law will become more and more important, even more so than your previous work.'

I took up my new post the next morning. The phone rang just as I was carrying my personal things to my new office.

'Congratulations, I heard you've been promoted to deputy-chief judge.' It was Dong's happy voice on the phone.

'Thanks. How did you know so quickly?'

'Who doesn't know in the bureau area? You're famous now,' she laughed. 'I'm also calling you about another matter.'

'What's that?'

'Do you remember that young man you introduced your friend to? Well, he's given me an answer already. He's not satisfied with your friend, he thinks she's too simple.' A couple of days ago, Dong had asked me to recommend someone for a young man who she claimed was of good prospects in almost every aspect, but who hadn't yet found a partner. I thought of a friend of mine and brought her to meet him as arranged. My friend thought well of him but the young man said he would give her an answer after thinking it over.

'That's okay,' I said hurriedly, 'I'll tell my friend. Bye.'

'Hang on,' said Dong anxiously, 'I haven't finished yet.'

'Make it quick then, I'm busy at the moment.'

'You promise not to be angry when you hear?'

'I promise,' I said, my suspicion mounting.

'He asked me to tell you that he wants to see you,' said Dong hesitantly.

'Why?' I knew it was a silly question as soon as I asked it.

'He said he's fallen in love with you.'

I'd guessed that was what she would say but I couldn't help laughing. 'Don't be funny! I'm only the go-between.'

'But he said he couldn't help being attracted by your charm when he met the two of you.' Dong was laughing now too. 'So you can't blame me for this, it's your own fault.'

'Have you told him that I wouldn't be a good wife as I have a strong career mind and spend most of my time on my work?'

'Yes, I told him you're a professional woman. He said that's one of your strong points. He knows you've been promoted and he says it's just what he admires. He likes successful women.'

It seemed I couldn't find any more excuses, but I still couldn't accept him. I asked Dong to pass on my appreciation for his admiration and apologise for my rejection.

Another call came in as soon as I hung up. It was President Lin, asking me to go to his office at once.

'You're really famous now,' Lin laughed before I sat down. I looked into his face but couldn't guess what he meant by that.

'I just received a phone call from the minister of the Personnel Department. He said you're being considered for the position of vice-secretary of the Committee of the Communist Youth League of the Nanchang Railway Bureau. The minister wants to hear your own opinion and give him an answer as soon as possible.'

'You mean leave the court?' I couldn't believe what he'd just said.

'Yes. It's another promotion, actually. The position is one level higher than your present position. Besides, working for the Youth League will give you a brighter political future. You know, Hu Yao Bang, the general secretary of the Central Party, was once a general secretary of the Youth League, and many important positions within the central government are now held by people who were secretaries of the league.'

'I understand your point,' I answered, 'but my career goal is not to be a high-ranking official or to have a bright political future, but to be a judge, just a successful judge. I don't want to leave the court.'

'Don't reject this so quickly,' warned Lin. 'Think about it carefully and give me a reply tomorrow. 'It's a rare opportunity – don't miss it.'

'I've given my answer already. I won't give up my present job.'

As I left Lin's office, I asked myself if I would come to regret the decision I'd made, whether I'd thrown away a good opportunity. I wasn't sure, but one thing I was sure of was that being a judge was my greatest desire.

I tried to forget what had happened and moved into my new office. The commercial division took up four rooms. The chief judge's office was bigger and had an inner room, which Chief Judge Qi occupied. Xiao Li, who was the office administrator, sat in the outer room. Qi asked me to sit in the outer room with Xiao Li. I gently refused and moved my things to the office I'd once used as a trainee. Tu Ke, Gao and Cao gave me a very warm welcome.

'It's so good that you've broken convention by being promoted without being a Party member,' said Tu Ke.

'But you'd better try your best to join the Party as soon as possible,' Xiao Cao advised.

I smiled without replying. In those days it was not easy to become a Party member. First I would have to submit an application and thought reports. I'd also have to have performed many good acts, preferably things that had been seen by others in the Party. I'd need a record of getting to work early and leaving late every day. Then I might be nominated by the Party group in my branch, after which all the branch members would analyse my merits and failings in my presence before voting by secret ballot. If I was lucky enough to win a majority of votes, my file would be sent to the Party Committee of the Railway Bureau for final approval. If approval was given, I'd be made a probationary member for a period of one year, and if I didn't commit any serious mistakes I would then become a full member.

There were twelve people in my division in the court and only four were Party members. Normally, being a member was the first step toward gaining promotion, and many young people in the court wanted to join the Party. But as the Railway Transport Court was strict about who could become a member, only one or two people were accepted each year, leaving a lot of people disappointed. Some old Party members created obstructions of every description, as they worried that young people would be promoted ahead of them once they became members. No one ever thought that I'd be promoted without belonging to the Party.

I suddenly felt very lucky and promised myself I'd work even harder in my new position.

面对干扰

FACING INTERFERENCE

Compared with criminal cases, handling commercial cases demanded a wider knowledge as every aspect of the economic field was involved. In keeping with the new system of reform and an increase in the number of regulations, the law was becoming an important means of regulating economic relationships and activities in China. The Railway Transport Court had been set up in 1979, and since then the number of cases handled by the commercial division had increased rapidly each year. In 1985 the division had received thirty-four cases, yet in the first three months of 1986 it had already received twenty-one. And as the government was emphasising the need for economic reform, the workload of the commercial division would continue to increase.

On that first day in my new job, I went to Chief Judge Qi's office to discuss my work.

'Sit down, I want to talk to you,' Qi said before I could open my mouth. 'How old are you?'

I was taken aback, not having expected such a question. When I didn't answer, he stared at me, smiling. 'Twenty-eight?' he asked.

'Twenty-nine in two weeks,' I replied.

'You're so young to be a deputy-chief judge. You should never be conceited or self-satisfied.'

'I won't.'

'You should still learn modestly from the old comrades, as they have richer knowledge and experience than you. And of course you lack social experience, so you'd better listen to the old comrades' opinions and advice, otherwise it'll be easy for you to make mistakes.' He glanced up at me. 'Do you have any knowledge of accounting?'

'No,' I answered. I knew he had ten years of accounting experience.

'What about railway transportation?'

'No.' As far as I knew, no one in the court had such knowledge, not even Qi.

'You see, you too have shortcomings, although you're clever and capable. You still have many things to learn. Right?'

'Yes, I will study hard in order to learn what I need to for my new work.' Although I didn't think I needed the knowledge he'd mentioned, I accepted that I had many things to learn. And I didn't want him to be displeased with me on my first day in the division. I learnt later that he was already unhappy with me because by taking the position of deputy-chief judge I had denied the job to Xiao Xu, his trusted follower.

Chief Judge Qi handed me a file and said, 'This is a debt case. Remember that it's a commercial dispute, not a criminal matter. You shouldn't hand down a judgement, but instead resolve it by mediation. Go ask Tu Ke to be the clerk.'

I could tell by his manner that as far as he was concerned our discussion was finished, and I left his office. He hadn't mentioned one word about the work I would be in charge of as a deputy-chief judge of the division. I returned to my office and told Tu Ke about the case.

'Did Qi ask you to try this?' she asked.

'Yes, you and me.'

'Didn't he put you in charge of some work of the division?'

When I admitted he hadn't, Xiao Cao and Gao put aside their work. 'But you're a deputy-chief judge now, not an ordinary judge,' said Xiao Cao. 'How can he treat you like this?'

'His patronising attitude has gone too far!' Gao's voice was raised. 'If I were you, I'd tell him he can't just assign me any old case, but must discuss the division's work with me. I'm –'

Tu Ke stopped him. 'Lower your voice, Qi will hear you.'

I felt depressed. I knew what Qi had done to me was unfair, and that what Xiao Cao and Gao said was correct. But if I did as Gao suggested, Qi would be angry and I would be scolded for not respecting the old comrades, or for being conceited because of my promotion, and that would be spread over the whole court. Chief Judge Qi would say that I looked down my nose not only at him, but at everybody. On the other hand, if I kept silent, he would continue to treat me like this. I hadn't anticipated such a negative start to my new job.

That evening I asked my parents what I should do.

'I didn't expect my daughter to be anxious about being an official,' my father laughed.

'Don't make fun of me, Father. I have no desire to be an official at all. I just feel I'm not being treated fairly.'

'In that case, you needn't care whether you are treated like a deputy-chief judge or not.'

'What do you mean?' I was confused.

'Your father's meaning is that you are still a judge and your most important work is handling cases, no matter whether you have an official title or not, no matter whether you are treated as an ordinary judge or a deputy-chief judge,' my mother explained.

'You're right, but I still can't help feeling a little unbalanced in my heart – he undermined me,' I muttered to myself.

My father understood and advised, 'Don't worry about such small things, but never make concessions on matters of principle.'

'Give in an inch and you will get a big yard,' I recalled my grandmother had once urged me, and I planned to give no more thought to the matter.

Next morning at work, Xiao Gao walked up to me and said, 'Chief Judge Wang –'

I cut him short. 'Don't call me that. Still call me by my name, please.'

'Okay, Xiao Wang, my daughter's got a temperature. Can I have half a day's leave to take her to the hospital?'

'Did you talk to Chief Judge Qi?' I asked.

'No. He's not in the office. Besides, you have the authority to give me permission, don't you?'

I thought he was right and agreed to his leave. Soon after

Gao had left, Qi came back and asked where Gao was. I told him I had given him a half day's leave because his daughter was ill.

Qi's face clouded over. 'How could he leave without letting me know?'

I wanted to say that I too had the right to give such permission, but I didn't. Instead I explained that Gao had wanted to talk to him personally but he was away.

My explanation didn't make the frown disappear from Qi's face. 'I don't believe his daughter is so sick that he couldn't wait for me to come back.' I zipped up my mouth so that I wouldn't say something to annoy him, although I myself was annoyed.

That afternoon, as I was reading case files, Xiao Xu shouted into one office after another, 'Come on, everybody! A meeting will be held in minutes!'

'What's the meeting about?' Judge Chen asked me when he passed by my office.

'No idea.' I shook my head.

Chen was surprised. 'How come? You're the deputy-chief judge.'

My face turned red immediately. What sort of a deputy-chief judge was I? I didn't even know why the meeting was to be held. I felt shame and vexation.

When all the staff of the division were in the meeting room, Qi announced, 'As happened last year, one member of staff in our division can receive the difficulty allowance. Today we'll take a short time to discuss who ought to be given it.'

Every year, in every work unit, a certain amount of money

was allocated for the payment of allowances to those staff whose financial situations were the most difficult. There was a quota for each section and it was up to the staff to determine who was most in need of the allowance. Particular consideration was given to those who had suffered unexpected hardships and sudden emergencies. The majority ruled when it came to making the final decision.

Xiao Xu spoke first. 'I think it ought to go to Lao Wu again as his family financial situation is the worst in our division. His wife has no job and is ill all year round.'

Xiao Cao put his own view. 'I don't agree. It's true that Lao Wu's financial situation is really bad, but the difficulty allowance is for coping with an emergency, such as a natural or man-made calamity. It shouldn't just go to the poorest, unless there is no one else in need of urgent help. I think Xiao Shen should be granted it because his mother-in-law died early this year and he had to borrow a lot of money.'

In China, people spent large amounts of money on funerals. As with weddings, they were big social occasions where it was necessary to have as elaborate a feast as possible.

Tu Ke and Gao agreed with Xiao Cao. Lao Wu said, 'I can't receive it every year. Please give it to someone else this year.'

Chief Judge Qi looked at everybody and then gave his own opinion. 'My suggestion is we give it to Lao Wu because his difficulties are lasting a long time. I think we must help in such cases. Regarding Xiao Shen's difficulty, his wife can apply for an allowance in her unit.'

In less than five minutes, Judge Chen and five others had chimed in with Qi's views. I didn't say anything. I wanted to listen first, as it was the first meeting I had attended in the division.

'All right, according to the majority view, I decide to grant this year's allowance to Lao Wu,' Qi concluded, and then declared the meeting over. He didn't care that I had remained silent. It seemed I didn't exist. This increased my sense of discomfort.

After the meeting, Tu Ke told me that whatever meeting was held, Xu always made a speech first which usually represented Qi's view. Qi would hope that other people followed Xu's opinion, and if so, Qi would make his conclusion last. But when, like today, different views were presented, he would hurriedly express his opinion. He knew that once he'd presented his view, few people would object to it because they wouldn't want to displease their head. In that way he would gain the majority and his view would always be the final decision, regardless of whether it was right or not. If it turned out that the decision was wrong and was criticised by the president or someone higher, Qi would say that it had been decided by a majority in the division.

Tu Ke also told me that the previous year, Cao had handled a debt dispute between a small private enterprise and a state-owned one. After three rounds of mediation had failed, Cao suggested handing down a judgement. At the meeting to discuss the matter, which was chaired by Qi, the final decision was for mediation. Qi advised Cao to maintain his patience with the mediation process and to try his best to resolve the case in that way. Then, after two subsequent attempts at mediation had also failed, the plaintiff, unable to keep his factory operating because of his unpaid debts, jumped into the Bayi River. When the president of the court criticised the handling of the case, Qi insisted that the decision to pursue mediation had not been his, but the whole division's.

I had a strong sense that my work in the commercial division would be no easier than it had been in the criminal division. But at the same time I was determined to defend my rights in my new position, not only for my own sake but for the sake of the whole division.

From that time on, no matter what kind of meeting was being held, I always tried to be the first to present my opinion on the matter under discussion. Gao, Cao and Tu Ke usually followed me and agreed with me. Those people who liked to echo their leaders' views would also express the same view as mine. In this way I always gained the support of the majority, and Qi would have to take the majority opinion as the final decision. But he would be so displeased that he would hope the practical implementation of the decision would prove the majority wrong, and he would be disappointed when he saw that the results were quite the opposite. After this had happened time and time again, Qi turned from undermining me to hating me.

In early July of that year of 1986, as the weather grew hotter and hotter, I felt dizzy almost every day. Finally I fainted in the office one day. The doctor put me in hospital and ordered further examinations, but I asked a court policeman to drive me home because I didn't want my parents to worry about me. My pale face didn't escape their notice, though and my mother prepared me two eggs with boiling water and white sugar – just as my grandmother used to do – and made me go to bed early.

I still didn't feel well the next day and stayed at home. At about two o'clock, as soon as my parents had gone back to work after lunch, Tu Ke arrived. She was anxious.

'Are you a little better? Qi suddenly asked me to prepare a discussion on the case I am handling by two-thirty this afternoon. I think he wants to hold the meeting without you so that his view will become the final decision.' (Tu Ke had been appointed a judge a few months before.)

'What's the situation of the case?'

'The facts and the evidence are very clear. It's the defendant's fault. I've tried mediation but the plaintiff refuses to participate and has asked that the court give a judgement as soon as possible. I reported this to Qi a week ago, but he asked me to persist with mediation. Three days ago, I raised the matter again and he said he would hold a meeting to discuss it. I didn't expect it to be held in your absence. You know such a meeting will be only a formality.' Tu Ke looked at her watch. 'You're sick, I can't ask you to come to the meeting, but . . .'

I knew well that she'd come to ask my help. I had a quick think and asked, 'You said the plaintiff refused to mediate, is that right?'

'Yes, I've tried to persuade his party several times, but they say they will only accept a judgement.'

'Okay, I'll come to the meeting with you. Let's go.' I stood up but had to stand still for a while as I was dizzy. Finally, with the support of Tu Ke, I got into the car. Ten minutes later, I appeared in the meeting. Qi was most surprised.

'Are you all right now?' He smiled, looking embarrassed. 'Wouldn't you be better having a rest for a few days?'

'Thank you.' I smiled back. 'I feel much stronger now.'

As soon as Qi had explained the case under discussion, I spoke up. 'According to the spirit of civil procedural law, the essential requirements for mediation are that the two parties agree to it and that there is a hope for and a possibility of reconciliation. Although we should stress mediation when handling a civil case, it's not compulsory. This is a law court, not a residential committee, and the legitimate interests and rights of clients cannot be protected if resolutions are delayed.' I looked around at everyone in the meeting. Many nodded their heads or smiled. 'So, if one party to a dispute is unwilling to mediate, a judgement should be given immediately, as long as the facts are clear and there is sufficient evidence to support them, which is the case in this instance.'

Except for Qi and Xiao Xu, everyone else expressed their agreement, one by one. Once, Qi would have put forward his dissenting view, hoping to win people over, but this time he didn't even express an opinion, saying instead, 'Since most of you think the case should not be mediated,' he stared hard at Tu Ke, 'you must act in accordance with the majority view. But I won't be responsible for it. Whoever handles this case will be responsible for it.'

Late in the morning of the next day, President Lin asked me to his office. I could tell from his expression that things were not good.

'I'm sure you'll be scolded,' Cao said.

'What for?' Tu Ke asked.

'Qi must have lodged a complaint against Xiao Wang,' Gao said.

'It doesn't matter. You have the chance to tell the president how unfair Qi is to you,' Tu Ke suggested.

'Don't worry, I know how to do it.' I gave them all a smile, though I knew they were right. 'Maybe the president wants to praise me.'

When I walked into his office, Lin's face was expressionless. I sat down a little way from his desk.

'We haven't had time to have a talk since you moved to the commercial division. How is your work going?'

I hadn't been expecting him to start in this way. Many things flashed through my mind, but I decided not to mention the conflict with Qi. 'Very good, I've learnt a lot from the work.'

'Right. You young people must constantly learn new things, and particularly from old comrades. They have much more experience than you.' I understood what he was getting at. 'You should respect them and listen to them. Don't think you can be arrogant and complacent because you've been highly educated and gained some achievement.'

I thought I should explain what had happened between Qi and me. 'I didn't, I –'

'Don't say any more. I know it all already.'

'That's only Chief Judge Qi's side. I hope you will also listen to my side.' I gave him the whole story without caring if he was listening or not.

After I had finished, he said, 'Well, you have understood what I meant. Everyone has shortcomings and anyone can make a mistake. Still, it would be good if you don't do it again. Okay, you can go back to work now.'

I was amazed at his comment and opened my mouth to speak, but said nothing. I returned to my office so full of grievance it made me want to cry.

'What did the president say?' Tu Ke and Gao came over to me. 'Did he criticise you?'

'No, nothing.' I tried to control my feelings.

After that, it took a long time to draw my mind back to the case I was handling. It was another difficult one. The defendant was a state-owned machine factory. One year before, it had signed a contract with the plaintiff, a collectively owned retail company, agreeing to make a machine for them and deliver it within four months. The retail company had paid a deposit in advance amounting to one third of the total cost of the machine. At the same time, the retailer had signed a second contract with a third party, another factory, guaranteeing delivery of this machine within six months. The dispute had arisen because the defendant, the machine factory, had not produced the machine by the deadline, and as a result the third party had cancelled its contract with the retailer. The retailer was now holding the defendant liable for breach of contract and was asking for the return of the advance and compensation for losses.

By this time, however, the director who had signed the original contract no longer worked at the machine factory, and the present director had declared he would not be responsible for any of the resulting debts. A clerk of the court had sent the new director a copy of the complaint against the factory, allowing him ten days to respond, but had heard nothing.

In order to ascertain all the facts of the case, I went to the factory with a clerk, Xiao Li. We met the director in his office, where he was quarrelling with a few people. A big, tall man in his forties, he asked a young woman to lead us to a small meeting room. Ten minutes later, he came in. He wore a factory uniform that was wrinkled and dirty.

'What can I do for you?' he asked.

I showed him my work card and told him I needed to ask him some questions relating to the case. He stood up suddenly and raised his voice. 'I've only been in charge of the factory for a month, I don't know anything about what was done by the previous director and I can't be responsible for what he did. You should contact him.'

'Don't get excited,' I said and asked him to sit down. I took time to patiently explain the situation to him. 'We will contact the previous director if necessary, however he is not the defendant in this case – the factory is, no matter who is the director. Whatever the previous director did, such as signing contracts, was done on behalf of the factory. Now that a dispute has arisen, the present director must be involved in its resolution, as a representative of your enterprise. Since you are the director now, we have to ask you to be involved. Of course, according to the law, you can authorise another person to do this, such as a vice-director or a lawyer.'

'I don't know the law nor do I want to know. I only know that the factory was run badly by the previous director and has incurred a great loss. My responsibility is to save the factory.'

'Well, the operating and financial situation of the factory is one of the things I want to know about.' I glanced at him, feeling his attitude had taken a turn for the better. Then I asked him some questions about the factory and the unfinished machine. He told me that it was half completed and still in the workshop.

'We can't return the deposit as it has already been spent on making the machine. The retail company didn't want it any longer, otherwise it would have been finished,' he said after I had explained the facts to him and advised that it was the factory that should take responsibility in the dispute.

'The fact is that your factory failed to deliver the machine on time, which caused the retailer to break another contract with a third party.'

'That's not my business. All I know is that we wanted to finish the machine but they didn't want it. So I can't be liable for it.' He stood up, his face on fire.

'Calm down!' I raised my voice. 'I have to talk to you in accordance with the law. Now, please cooperate with us.'

He sat down again, turning his head to the window. 'We have no money to compensate them. We can barely pay the workers' wages.'

'Well, you can try to discuss the compensation with the plaintiff, to find a way forward. But you must think about this seriously – either a mediation session or a hearing will be held soon,' I told him.

Xiao Li, who had been taking notes, handed two and a half pages to the director and said, 'Read this carefully and let me know if anything is incorrect. Otherwise, please sign at the bottom of each page.'

After a few minutes of reading, the director pointed to a sentence. 'I didn't say that, I said . . .'

Xiao Li amended the sentence as requested. Then the director objected to another sentence, and another – finally he asked Xiao Li to amend almost all of his comments. Xiao Li did her best to control her anger as she knew he was making things difficult on purpose. The director was no longer angry and he watched Xiao Li change her notes in triumph. But he didn't expect to have the tables turned so soon. Xiao Li gave the paper back to him with a smile.

'Okay, have another look. Are they correct now?'

'Yes,' replied the director.

'Now, you should stamp your personal seal on each word that's been changed, to prove it's you who changed it, not others.'

'I have no personal seal,' the director said.

'It doesn't matter.' Xiao Li took an inkpad out from her bag. 'Stamp it with one of your fingers. Here's the ink.'

The director looked at me. 'Must I do that?'

'Yes, you have to,' I said.

'But there are so many places.'

'That was at your request.' Xiao Li pushed the inkpad before him.

The director shook his head, put his forefinger on the inkpad and then pressed the places Xiao Li pointed to, one by one. When he'd finished, the two and a half pages were covered in his red fingerprints.

'Do you think I overdid it?' Xiao Li asked me when we left the factory. 'Actually, I needn't have asked him to certify every word, only a few long sentences.'

'Not at all. It's called payback. And anyway, we should uphold the dignity of the law before those who scorn it.'

Following our meeting with the factory director, we had a talk with the plaintiff at the retail company and his lawyer. Taking into account the difficulty of the factory director, the lawyer agreed to give up all demands for monetary compensation and just take the unfinished machine instead. I thought this was a reasonable compromise, but when I put it to the director of the machine factory he did not agree, arguing that the factory needed the machine in order to pay its other debts.

The retailer then submitted an application preventing the removal of the machine from the factory. As presiding judge, I had the authority to grant or reject such an application, but one thing made me hesitate. No one had issued such an order to solve a civil dispute since the commercial division had been established, and furthermore, I was not sure if the order could be executed successfully. I told Chief Judge Qi my thoughts, and he immediately objected to granting the application. When I insisted on holding a meeting of the division to discuss the matter, he said that such a major action should be reported to President Lin and a decision made by the judicial committee of the court. The committee was scheduled to meet three days later, but I didn't hold much hope that it would agree with my opinion, as the president was a conservative man.

On the day before the judicial committee was to meet, all the staff in the court were asked to gather in the courtroom. There President Lin announced that he was retiring that same day and that Judge Geng, who had been promoted to deputy-chief of the criminal division at the same time as my own promotion, would take up the position. Everyone was surprised at this news, and I was overjoyed as Judge Geng was totally different from Lin and Liu. Nearly fifty, he was open and above-board, upright and honest, full of legal knowledge and experience. I was sure the court would have a new face under his leadership.

As president, Geng didn't disappoint me. At the judicial committee meeting the following morning he approved my suggestion to grant the application to prevent the removal of the machine, although Qi tried very hard to persuade him and other members to accept his own view.

Two days later, I went with Xiao Li and three court policemen to the machine factory, where we struck trouble straight away. The director refused to put his seal on the relevant document and I was forced to ask the head of the workshop to do this instead. He was understandably reluctant but I convinced him that he would merely be acting as a witness to the machine being impounded. The court policemen then quickly sealed up the machine, marking it in several places with the words 'sealed' in black ink and with the court's red stamp.

'No one is allowed to touch this machine from now on, otherwise they will assume legal responsibility for it,' the court policeman warned once they had finished.

'I understand,' the head nodded repeatedly.

I took a deep breath now that the order had been enforced, but when we returned to the car and drove back to the factory gate, we met with further trouble. Dozens of workers were lining both sides of the road and others were leaning out of their office windows. Their strange expressions and smiles gave me a bad feeling.

Our car had to stop at the gate because the guard hadn't opened it for us. One of the court policemen got out but was unable to unlock the lock. He went to the guard's office, which had also been locked. The guard was not in. By then I realised what was happening and why the workers stood there smiling at us. They were waiting to have a good laugh at our expense.

I went to look for the director in his office but could find no one, and all the offices were locked. I suddenly saw how serious our situation was. We were unable to get out of the factory and we couldn't get help from outside since we couldn't get into an office to make a phone call. We might be facing more trouble than merely making fools of ourselves if we stayed there much longer.

'What shall we do now?' I asked everyone when I got back to the car.

'There's only one thing to do,' said one of the policemen. 'Smash the gate open.'

'Are you sure we can break the lock?' said the other. 'It's so big.'

'I've got a large hammer in my toolbox. It'll be no problem as long as Judge Wang permits me to do it.' They all looked at me.

Laughter had spread through the crowd. I had no time to think about things carefully. 'Okay, do it!' I ordered.

It took just two blows to smash the lock and our car was back on the road before the workers could do anything. We were joyous with our victory, and especially our exit, but I worried that what we had done was wrong.

While I was reporting the incident to President Geng, a phone call came in from the head of the Municipal Industrial Bureau. He was very angry, complaining that the court had sealed up the property of the machine factory, of which the bureau was in charge, without getting permission from him.

President Geng stayed calm. 'I'd like to advise you that the people's courts can take any legal action in accordance with the relevant law. It's not necessary to have permission from any administrative authority,' he said. 'I'd also like to advise you to educate your subordinates not to neglect the law in future, or to obstruct legal personnel who are carrying out their function in accordance with the law.'

I could hear that the head was in a thundering rage on the other end of the phone. President Geng kept a smile on his face. 'It's up to you,' he said. 'You can complain about us to whoever you like. We don't care as we haven't broken the law.'

'I'm sorry to cause you trouble,' I said after he'd hung up.

'No, you did a very good job. We need to give such bureaucrats a lesson in the law.'

I rejoiced that Geng was now the president and not Lin.

Here was someone who was willing to uphold the law, rather than trying to protect his own relationships with people. I hadn't had such a feeling of optimism since becoming a judge, and I thought my future must be easier now that there was such an upright and courageous court president.

外 国 原 告
THE FOREIGN PLAINTIFF

Handling commercial cases brought me into contact with a range of people at higher levels. Some were government officials and many of them were not used to being defendants. According to traditional Chinese thinking, being involved in a lawsuit was not respectable, especially if you were a defendant, and this was the case regardless of whether you won or lost. So when a summons was served on Director Hua, the head of the Department of Goods Transportation, he shouted, 'I don't want to go to court! I've never been a defendant before.'

The Department of Goods Transportation was the defendant in a case of damaged goods. The plaintiff was an American electronics company which was part of a joint venture in Nanchang. Joint ventures between Chinese and foreign companies had been made possible by the economic reforms of 1979, and since 1981 had become more and more common. The American company, by way of investing in the joint venture, had imported two very expensive pieces of electronic equipment that were to be used to manufacture electronic goods. This equipment had been transported from America to Jiangsu province by ship, and from there to Nanchang by train. When it was collected at the railway depot it was found to have been damaged. It wasn't clear where the damage had occurred, on the ship or on the train, but the law declared that, because the equipment had reached its final destination by train, the Railway Court had responsibility for the case, and for determining where the damage had occurred.

As the American company had suffered heavy losses, both direct and indirect, it had authorised a local lawyer to submit its complaint to the court and was demanding compensation.

'I'll give Director Hua a call,' Chief Judge Qi said when he heard that Hua had refused to appear at court for the case. 'He's my good friend.'

Late next morning, Qi asked me to the meeting room. Two people were sitting at the long table and they stood up smiling when I walked in. Qi introduced Director Hua and his lawyer. After greetings, Hua said he did not know the law and that his lawyer would have full powers to represent him in the case. Before he left, he emphasised, 'I'm Chief Judge Qi's old friend. Please look after our interests.'

I gave him a smile without a reply. Qi saw Hua out and said, 'Don't worry about anything.'

Only the lawyer and I were left in the meeting room. He was a middle-aged man with a pair of black-framed glasses which gave him an air of invincible solemnity. His name, Li Weilu, was well known to me, although I had never encountered him in the court – he was one of the most famous lawyers in Nanchang and had won many important cases.

'I feel fortunate to be working with you as I have heard of you for a long time,' Li Weilu smiled. 'Have you heard of me?'

'No, I'm sorry,' I lied. I knew what his intentions were in starting our conversation this way.

His face showed some disappointment but he recovered his smile very quickly and said, 'It doesn't matter. There's a saying, "Strangers at the first meeting and friends at the second." I believe we'll work together happily.'

'I hope so,' I replied. 'Tell me, what do you think of the case?'

Li's smile suddenly disappeared at my direct mention of the case. 'I'm the lawyer of the defendant, of course, so I need to protect my client's interests,' he said. 'The goods were damaged during transportation, but the plaintiff must take some of the responsibility for his package. It wouldn't be reasonable to ask my client to shoulder the full responsibility. Furthermore, my client is only the transport department in charge of the destination – the transport department in charge of the point of departure should also share the responsibility.'

'Do you mean your client is only willing to bear part of the responsibility?'

'Yes, at most one third of it.'

'The plaintiff will also bear one third?' I asked.

'Yes.'

'But an expert has examined the packaging. It complies with the standard for transportation, and the transport department at the point of departure hasn't claimed that the goods were damaged or the package broken when they despatched it. That means the damage could only have occurred during transportation, or with rough unloading at the destination.'

'Whatever it was, I hope the court will consider my client's difficulty and persuade the plaintiff to share part of the losses. A hundred and eighty thousand American dollars is a lot of money.' Li gave me a meaningful look. 'You know, Chief Judge Qi has the same opinion.'

'I'm sure he does but I'm afraid I can't accept it.' I felt uncomfortable.

'I've dealt with many judges, old and young, high- and low-ranking, but you are very different indeed.' He shook his head.

After Li Weilu had left, I went to give Qi my opinion of the case, which was that, regardless of whether the plaintiff was Chinese or a foreigner, the dispute should be solved on the basis of the facts and the law.

'It's true that rendering a judgement must be done strictly in accordance with the facts and law,' Qi conceded, 'but right now we're trying to resolve this through mediation. This can be flexible. Besides, when one party is a foreigner and the other is our state-owned enterprise, whose interests should we protect? You must try your best to persuade the American company to bear some of the losses.'

'I agree mediation can be flexible. I have no objection if the plaintiff is willing to reduce the amount of compensation, but I don't think we can treat foreign clients differently. That's not fair,' I argued.

'Why do you keep saying it's not fair? We are the people's

courts – shouldn't we protect our people's interests?' Qi lost his temper and shouted, 'You know, I've promised them we won't make them pay too much compensation. You want me to lose face on purpose! Why do you always want to do the very opposite of what I'm doing, again and again?'

His loud voice drew a few people out of their offices. I had a lot of things I could say in reply to him, but I swallowed them and went back to my desk.

That afternoon, I met Mr Brown – the plaintiff – and his lawyer in the meeting room. Mr Brown was worried the court wouldn't hand down a fair judgement as he was a foreigner.

'You can have faith in our court,' I said to Mr Brown. 'All people are equal before the law according to our principles. I will try the case on the basis of the facts and the law.'

'But Hua's lawyer told my lawyer that Hua had a good relationship with the chief judge of your division, and that the judgement would be unfavourable to me if I didn't accept mediation and give in,' said Mr Brown.

I did my best to reassure him. 'It's true that we prefer parties in a dispute to reach an agreement on the basis of mutual understanding and accommodation, but it has to be on a completely voluntary basis,' I explained. 'If there is to be a judgement, it will be made strictly in accordance with the facts and with the law. Nobody can place themselves above the law.'

Mr Brown stood up and shook my hand. 'You've set my mind at rest,' he said.

Once he and his lawyer had left, President Geng called me into his office. 'I've heard that you talked with the foreigner in English so that no one else could understand you. Is that true?' he demanded.

I was so surprised at how quickly someone had reported this that I could only ask, 'Who told you that?'

President Geng ignored my question. 'You had a good talk and finally you shook hands with each other, didn't you?'

In almost every work unit in China there were people who took great interest in watching other people's comings and goings, reporting every detail of their behaviour to the leaders and passing on anything they thought would result in someone being criticised. Such people seemed to gain some sort of pleasure and satisfaction from so doing. This wasn't the first time I'd been the brunt of people's nosiness and it certainly wouldn't be the last. I looked straight at President Geng to try and guess what his view on the matter was.

'Why do you look at me like that?'

'I don't think I did anything wrong,' I said. 'There are no regulations saying judges can not speak in foreign languages when they talk with foreign clients. I spoke in English just now because the plaintiff was an American.'

'Aha! You're annoyed!' His laughter made me confused. 'Okay, okay, let's be serious.' He stopped laughing. 'You did a very good job. The case will go more smoothly since you can talk to the client in his native tongue.'

I relaxed at these words and gave him the details of the case. I was so relieved I had his support once again.

'Do what you should do,' he said. 'I'll talk with Chief Judge Qi about this.'

The mediation was held three days later in the courtroom. Mr Brown's lawyer announced that he would be prepared to give up compensation for indirect losses (those resulting from income that would have accrued if the equipment had been in working order) as well as 20 per cent of direct losses (the cost of the damages).

'My client is willing to make this concession because he understands through his conversation with Judge Wang that the court will give him fair treatment. He is appreciative of it. Besides, he would like to maintain a good relationship with the defendant,' said the lawyer.

'What's your opinion?' I asked Hua.

Not having expected such an offer, Director Hua accepted it happily. 'I would like to say sorry to Mr Brown,' he said. 'We are accountable, regardless of whether the damage occurred at the departure station or the destination, and we have brought you heavy losses. We should bear the responsibility. I am moved by your magnanimous attitude and I accept your offer without any conditions. Furthermore, I'd like to offer to transport your goods free of charge next time and I guarantee you they won't be damaged again.'

'If you think the departure station would bear part of the responsibility, then according to the relevant railway transport rules you can request them to share the costs,' I advised Hua.

'Thank you for giving me a legal lesson,' he said.

Everybody was happy with the resolution of the dispute except Chief Judge Qi, who thought he had lost face before his old friend. He spread the news that he was unable to remain the chief judge of the division while I was there. He said he would apply for retirement unless I left.

'I know she has boundless prospects, but she is still young and lacking in experience, and she needs older people to lead her in the correct way,' Qi was heard to shout in the president's office. 'Since she has become so conceited, I can't work with her.'

The president did not accept Qi's complaint but instead asked him to try to cooperate with me, and for us both to appreciate each other's strong points in order to offset our weaknesses. This made Qi even angrier. He submitted an application for retirement to the personnel department, stating as his reason that he was unable to work with me because I did not respect him and submit to him. He reasoned that the personnel department would consider him the essential one of the two of us, as he was the older, more experienced comrade. The work of the division could not be carried on without him, and I would therefore be criticised and transferred to another division. I had no idea of this at the time, though, and did not learn of it until one month later when the news that Chief Judge Qi was to retire surprised everyone.

One morning in early October 1986, President Geng announced at a meeting of the whole staff that the personnel department had discussed Qi's retirement application and agreed to it. The relevant section of the National People's Congress had approved it and Qi would no longer be working for the court. 'Deputy-Chief Judge Wang will now be in charge of the work of the division,' said the president.

Qi was stunned. He had not expected to be defeated by a young woman, he said, and he refused to attend any farewell. He packed up all his personal belongings that morning and left without saying goodbye to any of us. Xiao Xu, Qi's faithful follower, kept silent all day. He knew he was in for a difficult time with Qi gone.

I couldn't help feeling secretly happy when I heard President Geng read the announcement, but I was suddenly rather disturbed when I saw Qi walking quietly past the window of my office. Looking at his old figure, I felt sorry for him. I associated him with my parents and I couldn't imagine seeing my parents experience such humiliation. Although I hadn't set out to confront him, I had hurt his self-esteem and his feelings and made him retire early.

When I told my parents that evening what had happened, they were surprised.

'Are you sure it was you who made him retire?' my mother asked.

'Yes. Everyone knows that.'

'How old is he?'

'I think he's fifty-seven,' I replied.

'That means he could have worked for another three years,' my father said, and sighed. 'I'm thinking you may have overdone some things in respect to him. He's an old comrade. You should have shown respect for him and given in to him over those small matters.'

'I did show respect for him and I only did what I ought to have done,' I protested. 'But he treated me as his enemy from the very beginning.'

'I believe our daughter has done nothing wrong but I still have sympathy for him,' my mother said.

At this Jing chipped in. 'Why do you sympathise with him? What would you think if his plan had succeeded and Ling had been criticised, or thrown out to another section? This is lifting a rock to drop it on one's own toes. He tried to harm others but harmed himself finally.'

'Enough!' My father stopped my sister and turned to me. 'We won't talk about this matter any more. You said you've been asked to be in charge of the whole work of the division, didn't you?'

'Yes.'

'So you must take some time to plan completely how you will organise every aspect of the work. Many people will be watching you. You must do better than Qi, otherwise you will disappoint the leaders who trusted you and the colleagues who supported you,' my father urged.

My mother said, 'One more thing I must advise you. You've had experience of being treated unfairly, so you must treat everyone equally, including those who once opposed you. As a leader, it's important to gain the support of all your staff. This is an art.'

I thought of Xiao Xu. My promotion had already destroyed his dream of being a deputy-chief judge, and Qi's retirement would have left him downhearted. How should I treat him? As well as I treated others? I felt a little ambivalent when I recalled his bad attitude to me. Besides, what would other people think if I treated him well? They might accuse me of making no distinction between friends and enemies. I lay awake all night, turning the problem over and over in my mind. It was much easier to deal with judicial work than with relationships between personnel.

The next morning, I moved to the office of the chief judge. I didn't take the inner room, in which Qi had sat, but asked Cao and Gao to put my desk in the outer room, and for Tu Ke's desk to adjoin mine so that it was convenient for her to assist me. All the file cabinets were moved from the outer room to the inner room, and the clerk Xiao Li's desk was moved in too.

As soon as we'd settled everything, Xiao Xu came in, stood before me and said without looking at me, 'Chief Judge Wang, I need a day's leave.'

For what reason? I wondered. Did he want a day of rest on the first day of my taking responsibility for the division? Did he ask this because of his low mood, or to express his dissatisfaction with me? His manner made me uncomfortable. I had been thinking about forgetting what he had done to me and treating him well, but unexpectedly he was making a protest to me. If I said no, it would increase his feeling of hostility to me. But if I said yes easily, it might be a case of *de cun jin chi* – me giving him an inch and him taking a yard. I had no time to think of a middle way, so just said, 'You can go if you really feel unwell.'

Xiao Xu glanced at me, then left without a word.

'See his disgusted look! You shouldn't have allowed him to go,' said Gao.

'Yes. If he dares to speak to you like that, later he will dare to climb over your head,' said Xiao Li.

President Geng, who had come in during this exchange,

said, 'How can this be so serious? I can understand Xiao Xu's present feeling. Actually, he is not a bad person. I think he can also be a valuable staff member, but it depends on how you mobilise his positive traits.'

'What should I do?' I asked.

'Firstly, you should clear up his enmity and make friends with him. Everyone has feelings. Try to move him.'

So that Friday afternoon, I held a meeting of the whole division. I asked everyone to sum up their work experience and say what they had learnt from it, and to discuss their future plans. While the others spoke eagerly, Xiao Xu sat with his head bent, saying nothing. I then requested that everyone be disciplined in their work, and after the meeting called Xiao Xu to my office. I wanted to say something encouraging to him, but when I saw his cold face I couldn't find the words.

'I know what you're thinking,' I said instead after an awkward few moments, 'and I understand your behaviour – that's why I asked you in here. I want you to know that I've forgotten the unpleasantness between you and me and I won't make things difficult for you, I promise. But I do insist that you not bring your negative attitude to work, and I hope you'll support me.'

Xiao Xu remained silent.

'All right, I'm finished. You can leave now if you have nothing to say,' I told him.

'I'll remember what you said.' He looked at me in great embarrassment.

One month later, Lao Yi, the chairman of the Workers' Union, announced that the court had received three new units of accommodation. In China at that time, accommodation was assigned by the workers' unions within work units. While rents were very low, there was an enormous demand because living space was scarce, and so whenever the court received new accommodation to assign, it was good news. Anyone who either had no accommodation of their own or whose accommodation was inadequate was eligible to be considered, and the union would rank those people according to their position, years of service, and number of family members.

Soon the union displayed the list on the noticeboard, asking everyone to check it in case there were any mistakes. I was surprised to see that my name wasn't on it. I knew that everyone of the same ranking as me in the court had already received accommodation as they were married and had children, and an employee's position counted for 40 per cent of the whole score. Combined with the score I'd be given for the other criteria, I should have been near the top of the list. I went to find Lao Yi in his office.

'Lao Yi, I'm afraid you left my name off the list,' I smiled.

'Come on, you don't need accommodation, you already have a big house to live in,' Lao Yi said.

'That big house belongs to my parents, not to me.'

'But you don't want to move out of it, do you?'

'Not at the moment, I don't,' I replied.

'So you don't need accommodation. I haven't made a mistake.' Lao Yi laughed.

'Yes, you have. According to the rules, anyone who hasn't got accommodation from the court is eligible to be considered,' I argued.

'But you don't want it.' Yi was growing angry.

'That's my business. You have no right to decide for me.' I didn't give in. 'As a judge, how can I protect people's rights if I can't even protect my own?'

'Okay! I'll add your name to the list,' said Yi vehemently.

'Thank you.' I felt satisfied.

The final stage of the allocation process was a meeting attended by the president, the chief judges of each division and the directors of each section. Yi announced that, on the basis of the assessment, the accommodation would be assigned to myself, Lao Zheng and Xiao Wang.

'Does anyone have a different opinion?' the president asked.

'Yes, I have.' I put up my hand. 'I suggest giving Xiao Xu the accommodation which was assigned to me.'

Yi couldn't help raising his voice. 'What are you doing? You insisted on participating in the allocation. Now you want to give it to another person.'

'That's right.' I smiled. 'I did that for Xiao Xu.'

'But Xiao Xu's score is lower than many others.'

'Yes, that's just why I did it. You may not know that Xiao Xu has a special situation. His wife was transferred to Nanchang City Bus Company from the countryside five months ago. Neither his wife nor his son's registration of permanent residence has been transferred to Nanchang yet, so when the union calculated his family members, there was only one. That's why his mark is lower than some others. In fact, he is the person who needs accommodation the most. At the moment he and his wife and son share a small flat with Xiao Xu's parents, a long way from here. As his wife works night shift every other day, they've had to put their seven-year-old son in the primary school close to our court so that Xiao Xu can drop him off and pick him up. As a result of our busy work, he often fails to pick up his son on time. The boy has to go home by himself when he doesn't see his father coming. It's twenty minutes' walk, too far for a little boy, and the complicated route is hard for him to remember. In the past few months the boy has got lost several times. Two weeks ago, Xiao Xu, as well as other people in our division, spent more than two hours trying to find him.' I looked around at everyone. 'So I think he is someone who ought to be given special consideration.'

My suggestion got everyone's consent, even Yi's, though he was still unhappy with me.

After the meeting, Yi announced the result to the whole staff and gave the keys to the three people.

Xiao Xu came to my office just as I was about to finish work. He stood in front of my desk saying nothing, but he couldn't stop smiling.

'Is there anything you want to say to me?' I asked at last.

'I just want to say thanks,' he replied, 'on behalf of my whole family.'

'For what?'

'Chairman Yi has told me everything. You have given my

family a great help.' He looked excited. 'I have been deeply touched by your magnanimity. I will repay you.'

'As a judge, I don't dare to receive your repayment, I'll be pleased if you just support my work,' I said with a satisfied smile. 'Let me know when you decide on a date to move. The division will assign a few young men to help you.'

After that, Xiao Xu's mood improved enormously and he worked harder. People praised me for my largeness of mind and leadership capacity, but I also received some negative comments. Someone said with a sarcastic tone, 'Xiao Wang is really competent. Who would have thought she could change Xiao Xu, Chief Judge Qi's faithful fellow, into her backbone?' Four years in the court had taught me that whatever you did, no matter whether it was right or wrong, would bring two kinds of comment. In the face of this I comforted myself with the old saying, 'Persist in your own way, no matter what others say.'

双重麻烦
DOUBLE TROUBLE

In the past, many cases had dragged on far too long because Chief Judge Qi had put undue stress on mediation. My way was to urge all judges to speed up their cases with judgements if they failed to achieve mediation. Besides engaging in case discussions with the judges, I continued to handle some cases myself, but the heavy workload and pressure made me exhausted. In January 1987 I went into a coma and was sent to hospital for blood tests. When the results came back, the doctor told me that excessive amounts of rectangular-shaped red cells had been found in my blood. Normally red blood cells are elliptical.

He turned to a page of a thick medical book and said, 'People who have such a condition may also have problems with their heart, liver, lungs and spleen, or have malignant tumours. So I suggest we do some further examinations on these organs.'

I did as the doctor suggested. Two days later, I got the results, which showed that I had no problems with my heart, liver, lungs or spleen.

'It's strange that everything is fine,' the doctor said.

'I have a clot in my thyroid gland. Do you think it's a malignant tumour?' I showed him the lump.

My question gave the doctor a start. He examined the lump carefully. 'Is it sore?' he asked.

'No.'

'Have you had any discomfort with it?'

'Actually, I've had it for such a long time, I don't know what it's supposed to feel like.'

'When did you get it?'

'When I was a little girl, at seven or eight. I can't remember.'

'Have you seen a doctor about this before?'

'Yes, quite a lot. I even spent a long period taking various traditional medicines, which were hard to take and not helpful.'

'Have you had any scans done?'

'About ten years ago.'

'What was the result?'

'It said it was a cold clot.'

'A cold clot?' The doctor was stunned. 'Are you sure?'

'Yes. It was recommended I have an operation, but I didn't because I was so scared.'

'I see,' the doctor said. 'I think you need to have another scan.'

I had a second scan the following Monday morning, and when I handed the doctor the report he knitted his brows. 'It's a cool clot, not much different from a cold one. You need an immediate operation,' he said determinedly, and wrote out a medical certificate. 'Go to the surgical department at once to pass this to the surgeons.'

'Is it benign or . . . ?' I didn't want to mention that negative word.

'Normally such clots are benign, but in this case it's hard to say. It may have changed because it's been there for too long. We won't know until we take it out and test it.'

'What if I ignore it?' I asked.

'You can't even think about ignoring it any more,' the doctor warned. 'It's absolutely essential to remove it. Even if it hasn't changed so far, it may in the future.'

I realised I had a serious problem with my health. But I didn't go to the surgical department and instead kept the certificate in my pocket and went back to my office. I tried to go on with my work but couldn't. I told Tu Ke I had to go home early.

'Are you all right?' She sensed something was wrong with me. 'Have you got the test results?'

'Not yet.' I left in a hurry before she could ask more.

I didn't go home but to a big book shop. In the medical section I found a text about tumours and read the pages relating to my disease. I learnt that there were four sorts of clots – hot, warm, cool and cold. They were all benign tumours, but about 15 per cent of cool clots and about 30 per cent of cold clots could undergo pathological change, into malignant tumours. Almost everyone in China thought that having cancer was equal to getting a death sentence. For a long time I couldn't move my eyes away from the words 'malignant tumours'.

I thought about my situation, the excess red cells in my blood, the doctor's shocked appearance, and I felt my road was approaching its end. My mind was all in a tangle. I didn't know if I should just leave the growth or have the operation. I had heard that if a clot was cancerous and was not removed cleanly during the operation, then the cancer cells would spread more quickly than if it was treated by other methods, such as herbs or chemotherapy. And yet I wouldn't know whether it was cancerous or not without having the operation. Though I had contemplated taking my own life in the past when I had felt too sad or that it was too difficult to live, I had thousands of unwilling thoughts when death looked like it might fall on me now. I didn't dare let my parents know the truth as I couldn't bear to frighten them. Without thinking clearly, I returned to the court with a heavy heart.

Tu Ke, Xiao Xu and Cao were just talking about me in my office. The president was also there. They gathered round me when I came back.

'I thought you were going home,' Tu Ke said. 'You look pale. Tell us what's wrong with you.'

'Was the scan test bad?' Xiao Xu asked.

'Show it to me,' said the president.

I took out the report and gave it to him.

They all stared at it. A few minutes passed before President Geng spoke. 'It should be a benign tumour. Don't worry too much about it.'

'The president is right. You'll be fine. Heaven stands by the good people,' said Tu Ke.

'The doctor didn't say it was malignant. He only asked you to have it removed. Don't frighten yourself,' said Cao.

I repaid them with a bitter smile as I understood they were trying to comfort and reassure me. President Geng urged me to see a surgeon the next day, then left after I promised him I would. I stayed in the office after they had all gone home. On careful consideration, I decided to take a bet with fate and have the operation. I would have no regrets if I lost because at least I would have tried. And maybe I would win, because I had grass fortune. I was the sturdy grass. I thought of the beautiful Chinese poem about grass withstanding the strongest fire, and reviving when the spring came. It was a severe winter already. I believed in spring's coming, and that fate would not be cruel to me.

Next day, I went to the surgical department and gave the report to a surgeon. He asked me to wait a while. After reading it, he asked me questions about my disease. More than ten minutes later, he came back with another doctor who was the director of the department. They examined me and discussed my condition, and then the director left. The surgeon told me that the director was prepared to devote great attention to my situation and had arranged the operation for the following Wednesday morning. The director would do it in person.

'Do you cough a lot?' the surgeon asked.

'No.'

'Do you have a cold?'

'No.'

'Do you have family in Nanchang?'

'I live with my parents,' I replied.

'Well, read this carefully and fill in the forms. Then ask one of your parents to come and sign them.' He passed me two forms. I knew that this was the normal procedure. It indicated that a patient had agreed to their operation and that the hospital wouldn't be responsible for any incident which might happen during surgery. Although I didn't think it was fair on the patients, I had to sign it. But I couldn't ask my parents to as I didn't want them to know the details.

'Can I sign it for my parents?'

'I'm afraid you can't.'

'Oh please, I'm worried that my parents won't be able to bear such a shock as they're old and not in good health,' I begged. 'Please!'

The surgeon had a soft heart. At last he allowed me to sign for my parents. 'However, you should let them know about the operation. You'll need to be in hospital from tomorrow for further examinations,' he told me.

'I understand.'

I went to the court to ask President Geng for leave. Then I asked Tu Ke to act in my place in my absence and gave her the key to the security box, in which was the stamp of the division and other important items.

'We may not need to use these things, you'll only be gone for a short time.' Tu Ke threw the key on my desk.

'Just in case I can't come back,' I said sadly, and threw the key back.

'Don't say those unlucky words,' Tu Ke said. 'You're making me upset.'

'Okay, I won't say any more.' I forced a smile. 'Let's talk about the unfinished cases.'

When we'd finished, I started to think about all the things I should do before the operation. I needed to make up a story to tell my parents. I needed to write letters to my good friends in other cities, but then I decided not to write to those who were married and had children – they already had too many things to be concerned about, I couldn't bother them with such potentially bad news. So I only wrote to one friend, Daijing, who was still single like me. And I needed to put my personal things in order and destroy my book of poems, my diaries and letters, many of which I had kept for years. I had got into the habit of writing my diary and letters during lunchtime and then locking my diary in my desk – I ate lunch at work because I lived such a long way from the office.

I carried all these things to the corner of the courtyard where Cao lit a fire for me. Most of my colleagues came to look while I squatted down to burn my private papers one by one. I had the feeling that I was leaving forever. I stood up, turning back to them.

'Don't worry, I won't burn down the building,' I joked when I saw their concerned looks.

'Don't you remember that Chairman Mao said a single spark can start a prairie fire?' someone said, trying to break the oppressive atmosphere.

No one else said anything. They just watched the flames.

My heart sank when I looked at my beloved things turning to ashes but I hid my feelings, smiling to everyone. 'Okay, it's all finished. You can relax now.'

'What time will you have the operation?' Judge Zheng asked suddenly. 'Let us know so that we can come to visit you.'

Everyone stared at me, waiting for my answer. 'At eight o'clock on Wednesday morning. You needn't come to see me, I'll be back soon.' I pretended nothing was serious. I turned and quickened my steps to my office, without turning back.

The most difficult thing, of course, was telling my parents. On the way home I thought out several ways to broach the subject, but wasn't sure which was best. That evening, I was distracted. I opened my mouth to tell them a few times but couldn't say a word until bedtime.

'Mother, I have something to tell you.' I stood beside her while she was having a wash.

'What is it?'

'I . . . I.' I couldn't go on.

'What's the matter with you?' My mother stopped washing and gazed at me.

'Tomorrow I'll be hospitalised because –'

'What did you say?' She was shocked.

'It's nothing serious. Just my thyroid clot.' I spoke lightly. 'I'm going to have it out next Wednesday.'

'Next Wednesday? Why did you suddenly decide to have the operation, and in such a hurry?' my mother asked anxiously. 'Are you all right?'

'Yes, I'm fine. I've thought about having it done before but

I've never had time. Now that work isn't as busy as in the criminal division, I want to take the opportunity to fix the problem.'

'Well, it's good to get it out.' I was relieved that my mother believed my story.

My father, who had heard what I said, asked, 'If what you say is true, everything will be all right. But don't hide the truth. Tell us if you're not well.'

'I will.'

My mother asked, 'Why didn't you tell us earlier? I haven't even time to prepare any food for you in the hospital tomorrow as there's a conference all day.'

'I can do that,' my father said.

'No, you needn't. Tu Ke will come with the car. And before the operation, I can order my meals from the hospital.' In Chinese hospitals, patients can only have meals sent to the wards at their own expense. Most patients had special, nutritious food brought to them by their families.

It was one o'clock in the morning by the time my mother had helped me pack up my clothes and toiletries. I lay in bed and looked around my bedroom, wondering if I would come back to it. I closed my eyes but couldn't get to sleep. I recalled my life, from childhood to working as a teacher, from studying at university to being a judge. I had tasted joys and sorrows, and had had more sour, sweet, bitter and hot experiences than most of my contemporaries. Now my road might end before I was thirty. On top of worrying, I regretted that I had not yet written down my life story.

I don't know when I fell asleep. I woke at seven, hurriedly

got up and had breakfast with my parents. They said they would come to see me at the hospital in the evening. From the black circles around their eyes, I knew they hadn't had a good night either, and I felt very sorry for still causing them so much worry.

On Friday afternoon, the third day after my admission to hospital, I was trying to finish a letter to my parents that I had been writing for two days when two men knocked on the door. The older of them, a tall man in a blue suit, told me they were from the Commission for Inspecting Discipline and wanted to talk with me. The younger man gave me an official document. I was puzzled as I knew the duty of the commission was to investigate officers of the state who had broken the law or violated discipline. There would be only two reasons for their coming to see me – either they wanted me to help them with someone else's problem, or I had been accused of something. From the expression on their faces, I had an ominous feeling it was the latter.

Just as I started to unfold the document, Xiao Cao and Tu Ke broke in. Cao snatched the document from my hands and asked the two men to come outside. He and Tu Ke then pulled the two inspectors out the door before they could open their mouths. About fifteen minutes later, Cao and Tu Ke returned. I asked them where the two men were and they told me they had made a mistake and gone already. Of course I didn't believe them. My years of judicial experience had taught me to see from people's eyes and body language if they were lying or telling the truth. I knew Cao and Tu Ke didn't want to upset me and were trying to hide something.

'Don't keep the truth from me. I'm already staring death in the face, is there anything more serious than that?'

They looked at each other and said nothing.

'Actually,' I went on, 'I've realised what's happened. It must be that someone has made a black report on me. I'm not afraid – a straight foot is not afraid of a crooked shoe. I haven't done anything illegal, so I don't mind their inspecting me.'

'Forget it. It's rubbish. We know you,' said Xiao Cao.

'The most important thing for you to do now is take it easy and recuperate from your disease. Leave other things for later,' said Tu Ke. 'You know, there are always some people doing dirty things behind others' backs.'

I appreciated their understanding and trust but I still wanted to know the details. 'Xiao Cao, give me the document. I need to know what it says.'

Hesitating for a moment, Xiao Cao took the document from his pocket and passed it to me. I opened it slowly and read. It was headed 'The Decision on Investigating Comrade Wang Ling's Accepting Bribes'. I held my breath and went on, reading sentence after sentence until a spell of dizziness stopped me. Xiao Cao took back the document while Tu Ke helped me to lie down.

'I told you not to read it,' said Tu Ke. 'We also got angry over it, as well as the president.'

'Does President Geng know about this?' I asked.

'Yes,' said Xiao Cao. 'The people from the commission came to the court to see him first and ask him to cooperate with them on the matter. He scolded them for deciding to investigate me without enough evidence and asked them to leave. The president's attitude annoyed the men, so they found out where you were from the guard. I happened to hear their conversation. I felt something unusual was going on and went upstairs to tell Tu Ke, then we reported it to President Geng. He asked us to come here to stop them. Just now, we told them you were having a major operation soon and convinced them to delay the matter until you've recovered.'

One misfortune comes on the neck of another. I felt deeply depressed. After Xiao Cao and Tu Ke had left, I was unable to finish my letter. I had too much to say to my parents and I couldn't say it clearly on paper. I tore up the unfinished letter and decided to write nothing. Standing in front of the window, I thought about what had just happened and wondered who wanted to set me up. The only evidence they had was a message on a greeting card someone had found in my office. It said, 'Chief Judge Wang, enclosed is two thousand yuan. Please accept it as a small way of expressing our respect to you and thanks for your just judgement.' It was signed 'Zheng Yi, on behalf of the whole staff of Jinyuan Trading Company, 8 December 1986'. I wasn't surprised that whoever wanted to hit me from behind had taken the card as a weapon, but I was disappointed that the commission had made a decision on the basis of such flimsy evidence, without any investigation.

Spring would be coming very soon. I hoped I could endure such a hard winter.

On Wednesday morning, my parents and Ping and Jing came very early to the hospital. Hui, who was then just fifteen, was still in high school, and my mother insisted she go to school that day. My friend Daijing, who had received my letter and arrived from Zhejiang province the day before, came with them. My heart was beating faster and faster as the operation time got closer. I tried my best to control my trembling and talk to everyone lightly. At eight-thirty, I wanted to hold each of them in my arms, but I was afraid they would see something unusual in this, as it wasn't the normal Chinese custom. Instead I just said, 'Time's up. I should go.' It was as if I were just going to work. They all stood up to follow me but I stopped them and asked them to stay in the ward. I thought that waiting there would be better for them than waiting outside the operating theatre. I gave a last glance at everyone, turned around and left quickly. Ping ran after me and walked with me to the operating theatre. We said nothing to each other on the way, but once we got there Ping suddenly held me, tears running down her cheeks. I controlled myself and wiped her tears. 'I'll be fine,' I comforted her. Then I pushed open the door and went in.

The operating theatre was a scary place. Everything was stark, drained of colour. The walls were white and the windows were hidden behind large white curtains. The operating table was covered with a white sheet, and laid out on a white cabinet by one wall were many medical instruments. Two doctors wore white coats and white caps. Several nurses wore white dresses and white caps. They all wore white gauze masks. So much whiteness made me dizzy, although white was one of my favourite colours normally.

A nurse asked me to put on a white patient's gown and lie down on the table. She put a white pillow under my neck so that my head was almost upside down, which made me uncomfortable and even dizzier. Another nurse came to give me an injection and soon I lost feeling in my neck. A few minutes later I was surrounded by the director, his assistant and the nurses. I was surprised at not being given a general anaesthetic, only a local one, but Director Feng smiled and said, 'So you want to go to sleep? You can't, you must talk to me.'

I thought he was joking but he explained that, as the clot was over my vocal cords, with a lot of blood vessels nearby, he wanted to be able to talk to me so that he'd know immediately if the vocal cords got damaged. The operation was a difficult one and I prayed to my grandmother to bless me in Heaven, to protect my vocal cords, otherwise I couldn't be a judge any more even if I did recover.

The operation started at nine. I felt the scalpel cutting into my neck but it was not painful. Soon after that, I felt a strange sensation on my neck.

'Are you in pain?' Feng asked.

'A little bit,' I replied.

'Do you need more anaesthetic?'

'No,' I said determinedly. I would rather bear the pain than have more anaesthetic as I'd heard that it was not good for the mind. I knew my mental health would be important if I survived this.

I tried to reduce the pain by diverting my attention. I kept my head still but focused my eyes on a big round mirror on the ceiling above me. I saw a person lying there covered in a pool of blood. I knew that it was me but fortunately, being short-sighted, I couldn't see my face clearly and was not scared.

About an hour later, I started to have difficulty breathing. When Liu asked me if I was all right, I answered him in a very weak voice.

'Get oxygen for her,' Feng ordered. Two nurses put a mask over my nose and I felt better immediately.

Another hour passed. By now I felt too dizzy to go on because my head was upside down. Feng kept saying, 'It won't be long.' Then, 'I'm sewing up the wound,' and, 'There are only two stitches left.' But those two stitches were taking forever and I realised that Feng had just said that to make me relax. In fact, he didn't finish the operation for another hour. He didn't wait for the nurses to take the bloodied sheet away but supported my back to help me sit up as soon as he'd finished the last stitch. As a result of getting up too quickly, I felt even dizzier, then I heard Feng's excited voice: 'Look! It must still be benign, it's smooth.' After a while, I could see that he was showing me a glass box in which there was a round lump about the size of a walnut. Though I'd only have the final result after the tests were done, I knew I'd walked away from the jaws of death. It had been a false alarm. I was so happy I hadn't let my parents become the victims of it.

I remembered Ping's words when I'd told her about my situation on the phone and asked her to take care of our parents. She said I should let them know the facts in case something tragic happened – they couldn't withstand it if it was very sudden. But I persisted with my view because I thought the earlier they knew, the earlier their sorrow would come.

After the nurses had cleaned me up, I was sent to a ward full of people. My parents, sisters, friends, President Geng and other colleagues were all waiting there. Before my stretcher got through the door, they all went into raptures, running to me.

'Don't worry about her. Everything is all right,' Director Feng said to my parents, and then turned to the others. 'What she needs now is a good rest. I hope you'll all leave soon. It's so crowded here that it's not good for her.'

'Xiao Wang's father and I are very moved to see you all here and very thankful you care for her so much,' my mother said to my friends and colleagues after showing her appreciation to the doctor.

They left for lunch. Xiao Huang, who left last, joked to me in a very low voice, 'Thank you, you've saved us the money for wreaths.'

I gave him an embarrassed smile. Fortune had played another joke on me. I couldn't help laughing in my heart for what had happened. Also, I was regretting having burned all my diaries and poems.

I still felt dizzy, and was also having great difficulty breathing because of a half-kilo sandbag pressing on my neck. Director Feng had urged me not to take it off, otherwise the blood vessels could break. But I had to remove it for seconds at a time to have a deep breath, then put it back again. I did this repeatedly, even during the night.

The next day Judge Shang and Judge Zheng came to see

me. After greetings, Judge Shang asked, 'What's all this about? Everybody in the court is talking about the Commission for Inspecting Discipline, saying that they've established a special group to deal with the issue of your taking bribes. It's said that President Geng is trying to shield you.'

'Who said that?'

Unexpectedly, the president came in just at that moment. He smiled and said, 'Take it easy. Regain your health. Put everything else aside until you recover completely.'

I was moved by his words, but it was hard to feel at ease while the problem was unsolved. I hated being the subject of widespread talk. Gossip was an insidious thing and it could completely undermine me. I asked President Geng to let the people from the commission come to see me. 'I can give them the company's address and telephone number in Chengdu. They can find out the truth from them.'

'They have the address and have already been there, but no one was there and no one answers the phone,' the president said. 'I believe in your integrity and I believe the matter will be cleared up later, but right now your task is to rest.'

After being nursed by my family with the best of care, I recovered quickly. As nurses in China only carry out medical procedures, and do not undertake general care of patients, such as washing them and so on, it's up to individual family members to do this, taking leave from work if necessary. Two weeks later, I was allowed to leave the hospital, but the doctor gave me a certificate of sick leave for one month. A few days after my discharge, with the consent of President Geng, Tu Ke and I caught the train to Chengdu, the capital of Sichuan province in the south-west of China, to visit the trading company I'd been accused of taking a bribe from.

A few months before, this company had been the plaintiff in a case I had handled. It had sued one of the Railway Bureau's factories for not paying for goods it had received. I had been unable to settle the case by mediation because the factory had claimed that it, in turn, was owed money by other companies and so could not make its own payments. I had then made a judgement in favour of the Chengdu trading company, which had initially been doubtful that its case would be given a fair hearing in the Railway Court. When the company had paid its court fees, it had included a cheque for an additional two thousand yuan, which I had promptly returned.

As soon as we got off the train, we went straight to the trading company, which was on the first floor of an old building. The door was locked and, though we knocked repeatedly, nobody answered. We went next door to try to get some information, and a man told us they hadn't seen anyone there since the New Year. We then went to the local Administration for Industry and Commerce, which handled the registration and disbanding of companies, and were told that the trading company's business licence had not been withdrawn and they didn't know what had happened to the company.

I felt so downhearted I didn't know what to do next. Tu Ke suggested we find accommodation and I was too tired to do anything but agree. Walking back past the Bank of China, I had a sudden idea: I knew the company's account was with the Bank of Industry and Commerce, maybe they could tell us its whereabouts.

Early next morning, we went to the bank and saw the director. He showed us several thick account books and told us that five years before, the trading company had borrowed two hundred thousand yuan and hadn't kept up the repayments. It had been given a six-month extension but still failed to pay, after which their funds had been frozen. Apparently the problem had been caused by a difficulty in getting payments from clients.

'Can you check the running account for last December?' I asked.

The director found the page. In the debit column for 6 December 1986 I saw an outgoing amount of two thousand, eight hundred and forty-five yuan to the Nanchang Railway Transport Court. I remembered that the court fees for their case had been eight hundred and forty-five yuan, and hurriedly checked the following credit columns. At last I found, for 20 December, an incoming amount of two thousand yuan, itemised as 'Returned from the Nanchang Railway Transport Court'.

Here was clear proof that I had not accepted the money but had returned it. I asked the director to copy the page for me and to certify it as a true copy. Back in Nanchang, I gave this evidence to the Commission for Inspecting Discipline, and about two weeks later, they issued a document formally revoking the accusations against me.

I swore that after the facts had been made known and I was back at work, I would find the person who had tried to frame me and teach them a lesson. But I never did, for several reasons. Mainly because I believed that good would be rewarded with good, and evil with evil. If the reward was not forthcoming, it was because the time had not yet come. And when the time came, I, and whoever had acted against me, would get our due rewards.

人 生 转 折

A DRAMATIC TURN

Early in 1988 the People's Supreme Court of China established a training centre for senior judges. Students were to be accommodated at Beijing University and eight at the People's University, also in Beijing. The aim of the centre was to improve the professional skills of judges, and participants in the two-year course were to be selected from all courts across the country by examination. I was excited to hear of this as I was always looking to broaden my knowledge. Since becoming a judge, my workload had been so heavy I'd had little time to continue studying, and I decided to sit for the examination without hesitation.

The procedure was complicated. First I had to submit a letter of application to the court, which President Geng then had to discuss with the Party secretary and comment on, before it could go to the personnel department for approval and finally the Supreme Court for registration.

President Geng, being an enlightened person, was pleased to see my application and delighted to support me. His recommendation convinced the Party secretary, and the first step went smoothly. But not so the second. The personnel department rejected my application on the grounds that I was already highly educated and in an important position, arguing that it was unnecessary for me to undertake additional study. Furthermore, they insisted, the commercial division needed me. Who would take my position in my absence? they asked President Geng.

The president agreed that the work of the division might suffer in the short term but that, with further study, I would be able to contribute even more to the court on my return. To which the personnel department replied that I might not even return to the Railway Court – I might stay on in the Supreme Court or go to the Higher Court – and wouldn't President Geng be sorry he'd let me go then?

He told them he would but that at the same time he'd be proud of me, and eventually the vice-minister of the personnel department relented. 'But don't complain to me later on when you have no one competent to appoint as deputy-chief judge,' he said to show his displeasure.

I was in a mediation meeting when President Geng called me to his office to talk to the vice-minister on the phone.

'Have you considered your application carefully?' he demanded as soon as I took the receiver.

I glanced at President Geng, who encouraged me with a smile. 'Yes,' I said, 'I think further study will be helpful to my work.'

'Your intentions are good but we think you're qualified for the work already. President Geng has suggested you be promoted to the position of vice-president of your court, and we've been watching you and are considering making the appointment.'

When the vice-minister failed to dissuade me with this offer, he grew angry and shouted down the phone, 'All right, I can approve your application but your position can not be held open for you while you're studying. You'll have to be reappointed on your return. I advise you to reconsider your application and give me an answer tomorrow.'

It was my turn to be annoyed. I hadn't expected him to try to block me by withdrawing my present position. I knew how many people coveted it and would be eager to take my place, and I also knew that plenty of others would have chosen the job over study, but I did not want to give up my ideals in order to keep a high position. And I resented being forced to make the choice. I controlled my rising anger and said, 'I can give you my answer right now. I'm willing to be reappointed when I come back.'

Once again I had paid a high price, but I had my approval at last. The news spread quickly through the court. Many colleagues were concerned about my stance. They thought it was unwise of me to leave such a good position and to have displeased the vice-minister only to take up study. But while some worried about my future and asked President Geng to give careful consideration to the matter, others were happy that an opportunity for promotion had been created. Someone even wrote to the president recommending himself for my job.

My parents were worried when they knew what I had done. 'Have you thought about what will happen if you fail the examination?' my father asked. His words made me uneasy. What if I did fail? I would have lost my present position for nothing. And how could I face the president and all my colleagues? How could I face the vice-minister? I suddenly felt an enormous pressure, and I had brought it all upon myself. Should I give up now? No, I couldn't. Others would think I was afraid of losing my official position. I had no choice but *bei shui yi zhan* – to fight with my back to the wall.

Besides working at the court as usual, I made good use of my limited time to prepare for the examinations. For about four months I got five hours' sleep a night, but my reward was good marks and a letter of offer to enrol at the centre. The exams had been held at Beijing University over three days and I hadn't found them too difficult.

In August of 1988 I transferred my workload to Tu Ke, who had been promoted to deputy-chief judge of the division, just as I had recommended, and started a Masters degree majoring in commercial law at Beijing University.

The day before I left, I got a phone call from the minister of the personnel department, who had just got out of hospital. He gave me his congratulations and urged me to study hard and come back once I'd graduated. He told me he regretted the vice-minister's attitude toward me and that my position would be kept for me. I was so moved I assured him I would do as he hoped.

Becoming a student again after ten years was revitalising. The situation in universities was very different now, much freer and more open. More and more foreign lecturers were being invited to teach in China, and more foreign students were also studying there. Cooperation between Chinese and overseas universities had strengthened and it was much easier for Chinese students to go overseas to study. Compared with the judicial work in the court, my study was more theoretical and covered a wider area, encompassing economic legislation and the administration of justice. I didn't regret having taken the option of studying – far from it; I hoped to get a chance to go abroad to learn about the judicial system in Western countries.

The opportunity came along in 1989. The centre announced that the American Ford Foundation would sponsor seven students to study in America and other English-speaking countries for one year. Once again, selection would be by examination, and as language was the most important criterion for studying abroad, English was the only subject. The exam comprised a written and an oral section and competition was keen, as most of the students at the centre were taking it. Although I had studied English for four years at university, I'd had few opportunities to practise it in recent years and had forgotten a lot, whereas students from places like the Supreme Court and the maritime courts regularly used English in their work.

But when I got the results I found I'd come second in the written test and third in the oral and was the only judge selected to go to Australia. The six other successful applicants were all male and were sent to America, Canada and England.

On the first of May I went back to Nanchang to share this good news with my parents and sisters. But as soon as I stepped into the house, I felt a gloom hanging over it. Ping and Jing, who were both married by now and living with their husbands, were there and Hui, I knew, was at school. There was no sign of my parents.

'Where are Father and Mother?' I asked.

'Sit down.' Ping drew me to the sofa. 'Have you had your lunch?'

I nodded and looked around at Jing and my brothers-in-law. 'What's wrong with you? Where are Father and Mother?'

My sisters started crying. I had a sense of a great disaster waiting to happen. 'Tell me!' I shouted, standing in the middle of the room. 'What's wrong with Father and Mother?'

'Your father and mother are at the hospital,' my elder brother-in-law Meng finally replied.

'The hospital?' I repeated stupidly.

'Yes, your father has cancer of the pleura. He's having an operation in a week, next Friday.'

I fell down onto the sofa, feeling as if a bucket of cold water had been poured on me. I could not believe what I'd heard. 'How can it be? Are you sure it's cancer?' I asked Ping.

She nodded. 'The doctor said it has reached an advanced stage.' Ping was still crying. 'I don't know if he should have the operation or not.'

'Does Father know it's cancer?'

'No, we haven't told him. We were just discussing it. I think hiding the truth is good for him.'

'I agree with you,' I said. I'd heard that many cancer patients' spirits broke when they knew what disease they had, causing them to die more quickly.

'I think we also need to hide the truth from your mother. I'm afraid she won't be able to bear it,' Meng suggested.

After further discussion, we decided to tell our parents that Father had a benign tumour, and to ask his doctors and nurses to cooperate with us. We'd need to get a false test result to show Father.

Ordinarily I hated to beg others to do anything for me, but at such a time I threw my shyness away and knocked on the door of my father's doctor, who was famous and known as 'the first scalpel' in Jiangxi province. He sympathised and promised to do what I requested. Ping arranged for the false test report from the X-ray department, and once everything had been arranged, my sisters and I went to see our father in hospital.

My mother was sitting beside his bed, massaging him gently. I was sad to see his pale face and my mother's worried appearance. Both of them were very pleased to see me back, and especially pleased on hearing my good news.

'I'm so happy to hear that. I'm proud of you,' my father smiled. 'But Father may be unable to see you off.'

'Don't say that. The result has come out. Like mine, it's benign. After the operation you'll be fine, and the pain will disappear.'

Ping gave the report to my father. My mother passed him his glasses and he read it carefully, then said, 'I hope it's correct, but I shouldn't feel so sore if it's benign.'

'Father, I'll tell you a secret.' I told him how my doctor had suspected that the clot in my neck had changed into a malignant tumour, and the silly things I'd done. 'Don't frighten yourself as I did, please.'

This story surprised my parents, but also relaxed them to some extent. My mother smiled and said to my father, 'Listen to your daughter, and don't give way to foolish fancies.'

'All right, all right.' My father turned to us. 'I'm so sorry to cause you worry.'

We sisters looked at each other, feeling terribly upset but not daring to appear so. At the same time we felt uneasy about our lies, but I knew that Heaven would not punish us as they were based on goodwill.

I did not go back to university after my father's operation as classes had all but stopped as a result of a student protest which was agitating for increased democracy in China. The pro-democracy movement, which was to culminate in the demonstrations in Tiananmen Square in June 1988, had intensified since May. But the main reason for my not returning was that my father's situation was worse, even though the operation had gone smoothly. Two weeks after it, before the pain caused by the surgery had gone away, he felt a new pain in his chest. Test results showed that another cancer had grown. The doctor told us that the only remaining options were chemotherapy and radiotherapy, but that they wouldn't be much help as the cancer was too advanced.

This news was like a blow to the head. We didn't tell our parents, saying instead that Father had an infection. After further discussion, my sisters and I decided against chemotherapy as it was too damaging to healthy body cells. We opted for radiotherapy and also began actively looking for alternative ways to treat him.

We found a traditional Chinese doctor with a lot of experience in this field who agreed to try to maintain my father's life for a little longer. I begged him to do his best to keep my father alive at least until I returned from overseas. He wrote out a prescription for more than ten kinds of Chinese herbs and said he would come to see my father once a week in case he needed to adjust the prescription. Meanwhile I found a qigong master – qigong is an ancient system of deep-breathing exercises – and we told my parents that the infection had been caused by my father's lack of strength, and that qigong would build up his resistance to disease.

Days passed and my father's condition was getting worse. His pain increased and soon it was lasting twenty-four hours a day, which meant he was unable to eat or sleep well. The painkillers he had been having no longer stopped the pain, and when the doctors saw him suffering so much they gave him a much stronger drug called Dolantin. In the beginning, this would ease his pain for three or four hours, but soon its effects wore off after only an hour, then half an hour. Because this drug was dangerous in large quantities, my father would still have to wait four hours until the next injection, and in the meantime he had to endure severe pain. He was getting weaker and weaker and couldn't stand up without help; then he couldn't sit up, and finally he couldn't even turn over in bed. Looking at this thin face full of suffering, I felt as if a knife were piercing my heart. I hated that I was unable to help him or share his pain. I wished I could take his place.

I shall never forget one night in particular. I had been at the hospital for over twenty-four hours straight – I was spending more time looking after my father so that my mother and sisters need not ask for leave. After an injection, his pain reduced a little, my father said to me in a very weak voice, 'Ling Ling, you need sleep. You can't stay up for another night, it will affect your health.'

'Don't worry about me, I'm not sleepy,' I smiled. But my father persisted and I had to obey him. I lay down in another bed and closed my eyes, pretending to fall asleep. About half an hour later, I heard my father groaning again. It was lower than usual because he was afraid he'd wake me up. My heart ached at having no way to help him. I got up and said, 'Groan loudly, Father. You may feel better.'

'I'm sorry to have woken you. I tried my best to control myself.'

'No, you needn't do that.' I squatted beside his bed and massaged his forehead, trying to take his attention away from the pain. Two hours passed. It was one o'clock. My father's groans were getting louder and his shirt was soaked through with sweat. I took out another one to change him but he stopped me.

'It's not necessary. It will only be drenched again soon,' he said sadly. 'Can you ask the doctor to give me another injection?'

'But it's only been three hours since the last one. You can't have so many injections, they have dreadful side effects.'

'I know, but I can't stand it. Please!' he begged.

'Father, it isn't that I want to see you suffer so much, but Dolantin is really bad for you.' I fought back my tears.

He looked at me then and said, 'I know I have cancer, although you don't want me to know. I appreciate your and your sisters' goodness, but I'm clear about my disease. I haven't got much time to live. Don't let me suffer from the pain, all right? Father begs you. Ling Ling, please!'

His sad words and begging eyes made my heart break. I couldn't hold back from crying any longer. A man of iron, who hadn't fallen down on battlefields, who hadn't buckled during political movements, was now defeated by the demon of disease. I hated that fortune was so unfair to my father. I got down on my knees, choking with sobs. 'Father, please forgive your daughters' incompetence in not being able to reduce your pain. But we are still looking for alternative ways to treat you. I beg you, don't ask for too much Dolantin, please!'

My father gently patted my head and said in a tearful voice, 'Don't cry, Ling Ling. Your crying makes my heart ache. I won't ask for the injection. I'm sorry, it's all my fault. Get up, please.'

No words could express my feelings at that time. I was torn between wanting to ask the doctor to give my father an injection whenever he was in pain, regardless of how often, and not wanting to risk damage from the overuse of Dolantin, should his life be saved. I watched his suffering with bleeding in my heart, before finally going to ask the doctor for another injection. By then my father had already endured another hour.

Although we had found several ways to treat my father's pain, none was helpful. One morning, I got a letter from the training centre saying that the six other students had gone overseas already. The centre hoped I could submit a visa application soon. Once again I faced a hard choice: my career or my father. It would be a pity to give up an opportunity to study overseas, which was not easy to come by, but how could I leave my father? I would regret it all my life if he wasn't alive when I came back. My father and mother had asked me to return to university many times, and now my father said he wouldn't feel easy if his health affected my career. My sisters and brothers-in-law also tried to persuade me to go, saying that they would look after him in my absence.

'You'll still be unable to save Father if you give up your future, and it will only make him more upset,' said Ping. 'I think you'd better go soon, so that you can come back earlier. Maybe you can find some effective medicine in Australia.'

I thought she might be right, but I still didn't want to leave until I saw my father getting better. In the end, I didn't wait for such a day. On 7 December 1989, seven months after my father's operation, I went back to Beijing to apply for a visa. My father was still suffering greatly. The train departed at six o'clock in the afternoon and I only left the hospital at five-thirty.

Before I left, my father gave me some advice. 'It's not easy to get the chance to go overseas to study. You must cherish this opportunity and make good use of your time,' he urged. 'Learn new things. And pay attention to your health – take care of yourself when you're away so that we won't have to worry about you.' He looked at me. 'You're more than thirty now, and still single. That's the main thing stopping me setting my mind at ease. I hope you will consider your personal life too, when you're in

Australia, since you won't be as busy there as you were in the court.'

I controlled myself and did not cry, but listened to him carefully and promised him repeatedly that I'd do as he said, nodding my head. We said goodbye with smiles, but hardly had I moved my legs out of the ward when, in the corridor, I threw myself on my knees towards the direction of my father, making kowtows to him, wishing I could find good medicine for him and hoping he would be there on my return. Then I rushed out of the hospital and got into the car the court had sent for me, crying loudly all the way to the station.

I did not expect that this goodbye would be our last. Those final encouraging words were my father's last to me. Twenty days later, while I was still waiting for a visa in Beijing, he died of heart failure. I was too shocked to say anything on the phone when Meng called to give me the news. Tears could no longer express my sorrow. I deeply regretted that I hadn't stayed at his side in his last days. I couldn't forgive myself for having been so concerned with my career. If I could have gone back in time, I would have stayed with him every minute.

I returned to Nanchang immediately to pay my last respects. My mother had fallen into a coma three times and Ping had been keeping watch by her bedside. Meng advised me to control my sorrow, saying, 'You must contain your grief. You need to organise the funeral and deliver a memorial speech on behalf of us. Ping is unable to do it.'

Looking at my sisters, I understood I must bestir myself to shoulder the load, and I forced myself to bury my grief in my heart. With tears in my eyes, I wrote a speech, arranged everything for the funeral and received visitors. Several times I almost collapsed. I finally did faint when I saw my father's body being sent for cremation. Before then I still had some fantastic notion that he might revive, but at that point my hope crumbled. I had to accept the cruel fact that my father was gone forever.

告别过去
SAY GOODBYE TO THE PAST

Seven months later, I finally got a visa from the Australian embassy in Beijing, and in August 1990 I left for Australia, with deep thoughts of my father and great concern about my mother. I did not return to university for those seven months since there were still no classes, as a result of the events in Tiananmen Square. I did not go back to work either, but spent that time taking care of my mother, who was sick with grief. My father's death had affected her deeply, and when my visa was granted at last it was hard for me to leave her. She retired from work and went to live with Ping for a year after I left, before eventually returning to her own house.

I flew to Melbourne and was met by someone from the Asian Law and Business Centre at the University of Melbourne, where I was to be based. As soon as I walked out of the airport, I felt the fresh Australian air, the strong sunshine, the blue sky. It was winter but I didn't feel cold. Every leaf on the trees looked so clean – as if they had just been washed. I asked if it had been raining and learnt that it had been fine for many days, but apparently many Chinese have this same feeling on first coming to Australia.

We drove down the freeway to the city and I was struck by the green land stretching as far as I could see, until it connected with the horizon. The traffic was very fast, but orderly and quiet. As we got closer to the city there were fewer high buildings than I'd imagined, but I still felt the city was beautiful.

It had been arranged that I would live in a suite at International House, which provided accommodation for overseas guests and students at the university. The rent covered a cleaning service and three meals a day – Western food, of course. When I went to the Asian Law and Business Centre the following day, only my second day in the country, I was already desperate to eat some Chinese food, and was thrilled to learn from a coleague that I could buy almost anything I wanted at Chinese groceries.

So that I would have more chance to improve my English and be able to cook myself Chinese food, I decided to live in an Australian household. On the university noticeboard I saw an advertisement for a room in a house nearby. I phoned and discovered that the owner was a kind woman in her fifties named Janet, whose husband had died and whose children had left home. The first thing I saw when I walked into her house was a scroll with Chinese characters. It turned out that Janet had a great interest in China and was a member of the Australia–China Friendship Association. But her simple old furniture and her fourteen-inch black-and-white television surprised me. I thought everyone in foreign countries had newer televisions than Chinese people had. By the time I left China, most people had television, and most people in cities had large-screen colour sets.

Janet and I reached a rental agreement immediately and I took a room in the front of the house. It was also simple, but clean. The rent was reasonable for Melbourne, but compared to China it was too expensive to believe. In Nanchang my family paid only a few yuan (about one Australian dollar) a month for a hundred and twenty square metres, and here for this small room I had to pay almost fifty times that much per week. But while accommodation in Australia was dear, food was cheap. Chinese people spend about 70 per cent of their salaries on food, whereas Australians need spend only a small part of their income in order to eat.

I was welcomed warmly by the university and had an office there. I was not enrolled in a formal course of study but was able to do my own research and attend seminars and business functions. At that time, economic activity between China and Australia was booming, and I was frequently asked to explain points of law relating to doing business in China. But even the feeling of being in a new place and being busy with study and social activities couldn't make me forget my sorrow. For a long time, I cried quietly in bed at night. I couldn't help missing my father and I worried about my mother. I rang her almost every week.

After a few months of research into the Australian legal system, including two weeks in the Commercial Division of the Supreme Court of New South Wales in December 1990, it was clear to me that the Australian and Chinese law and court systems could not be more different. While I studied the Australian legal system, I also introduced the Chinese legal system to

Australian judges and any other legal professionals who were interested. Many people were surprised to hear that I was a judge – they thought I was too young. I was often invited to attend parties and conferences and whenever anyone said, 'How can you be a judge? You look too young,' I would reply, 'I'm just a very lucky woman.'

Besides meeting a lot of Australians, I also got to know Chinese people who were studying or working in Melbourne. It was at the Melbourne Magistrates Court that I met Dingda. We were both there for the same case, which involved two Chinese students. One was his friend and the other was mine. His friend asked him to be an interpreter and mine asked me to be his legal consultant, even though I still knew little about Australian law. Dingda was from Jiangsu province and had been in Australia for over a year. He was working for a Chinese trading company and he was tall and full of vigour and vitality, the kind of young man who easily attracted girls. He wore a grey suit with a silk tie to match, and his black hair was bright and tidy. We didn't talk much in court but afterwards he gave me his business card and asked for my phone number. Out of politeness I gave it to him, but I did not expect him to ring me that same evening.

After that he often rang or visited. I didn't see anything unusual in this as he was not the only person to do so. Being in a foreign country, it was natural that we'd seek out other Chinese people to ward off loneliness. And I enjoyed such friendships – through them I learnt about many aspects of Australia I otherwise might not have.

Except for missing my father and family, I was finding

Australia a relaxed and pleasant place, but this wasn't consistent with my fate, which always seemed to have a mishap in store. In March of 1991 I had an accident in Janet's car. I was sitting in the front passenger seat when another car ran into us from the left. With the sound of the crash I felt a bump on my head and blood flowing down my face. I was dizzy and unable to open my eyes.

People crowded around the car. I heard someone ask me anxiously, 'Are you all right? I'm a doctor. Can you speak to me?' I wanted to say something but I was too weak to open my mouth. I felt like I was spinning in mid-air and I couldn't see – I thought I was blind. Some time later, two people from the Royal Melbourne Hospital helped me out of the car. They told me the ambulance had arrived and I would be put into it on a stretcher. I refused and tried to stand up but couldn't.

In hospital, the blood was cleaned off my face and the bleeding stemmed. I had a cut from the middle of my forehead to the corner of my left eye. Fortunately, my eyes hadn't been damaged but I was found to have cerebral concussion. I stayed in hospital for about eight hours, and a nurse came regularly to ask me my name, age, the date and where I was.

As a result of the concussion I was constantly dizzy and couldn't do any reading or writing. In order to make up the time I would lose from my placement, the university helped me get permission from the Supreme Court of China to stay in Australia for another six months, and as I couldn't study I decided to do some travelling. At that time it was not easy for Chinese people to get permission to go abroad, and since I was already overseas

I wanted to take the opportunity to visit other countries and see how people lived. I chose Eastern Europe as I wanted to know what other socialist countries were like.

Since the car accident, Dingda had been contacting me more often. When I told him my plans, he asked, 'Is anyone going with you?'

I told him no one was and without hesitating he said, 'Well, I'll go with you.'

'Why?' I asked, surprised. 'You have to work.'

'It doesn't matter. I can't let you go alone. I'll worry about your health, and your safety.'

'Come on!' I laughed. 'I'm not a child, I can look after myself.'

'I must go with you, otherwise I won't be able to sleep properly.'

Again I was surprised, both at his words and his serious expression. He might have a special feeling for me, I thought, but I wasn't willing to think about that. He was nine years younger than me and I had been treating him like a younger brother. Since he didn't say anything more, I pretended not to understand. 'Okay,' I said lightly. 'It's up to you.'

Ten days later, we flew to Budapest, the capital of Hungary. We found a hotel in the centre of the city. Dingda indeed acted as both a brother and a guard. He was extremely thoughtful, showing me every possible consideration and looking after me with great care. But happy as I was to have such a good friend, I also felt uneasy. I was afraid he would express his real feelings, and whenever his conversation seemed to be going in that direction, I hurriedly changed the subject. We stayed in Hungary for two weeks, and every day was a joy. We talked so much – about China, other countries, our lives, careers, hobbies, interests, families, friends, the past and the future. We had so much in common and I felt I came to really understand him. His life experience was a lot richer than most people his age, making him more mature.

We'd planned to go to Czechoslovakia after Hungary, but while I was able to get an entry visa from the Czech consulate in Budapest, Dingda could not. He was told he'd have to apply in Beijing since he held a private passport, which was issued to people who went abroad for personal reasons, while I held a service passport, issued to those who were sent by the state. So I decided to take a day tour by myself to Prague.

Dingda came with me to the train station, and before leaving he passed me a folded sheet of paper, saying, 'Don't open it until the train leaves.' I held it in my hand as I watched him disappear in the crowd, then I hurriedly unfolded it. To my surprise it contained two lines of poetry. He hadn't expressed his affection for me but I had a premonition that this was only the first step.

Back in Budapest, I didn't mention the poem. I pretended nothing had happened, even though Dingda kept his eyes on me constantly, expecting me to say something. His expectation soon turned to disappointment.

On the morning we were to return to Australia, he came into my hotel room with a gloomy expression. I was writing my diary and he was quiet for a while, then he said suddenly in a serious voice, 'Marry me, please. I know I don't deserve you. You're a successful woman and my career is just beginning, but I promise you I'll try very hard to be a success.' He glanced at me. 'I really love you, though I have been scared to say this. I've never had such a strong feeling for a woman before. Last night I was thinking all night. No matter whether you accept me or not, I must ask, otherwise I'll regret it all my life.'

I listened to him in silence, not knowing what to say. My face was burning, my hands were shaking and my heart was beating fast. I put down my pen and lowered my head. I didn't dare look into his eyes so full of emotion.

'Say something please, just yes or no,' he begged.

But it was hard for me to say yes or no. I couldn't say yes as I was afraid we were unsuited for marriage because of the age gap between us. I was afraid he was just being impulsive and his love wouldn't last. And I couldn't say no because he had proved by his behaviour that he really loved me, and he had made me very happy in the past days. And what's more, I'd fallen in love with him. During my day in Prague his presence was always with me, no matter how hard I tried to push him away.

Even though I wasn't looking at him, I felt his eyes on me. He was waiting for my response. I must give him a clear answer. After hesitating a long time, I asked a question of my own rather than answering his.

'Have you considered my age? I'm nine years older than you, not a small gap. You might meet a younger woman you like better one day. Then you'll regret marrying me.'

'No, I shall never regret it. In my eyes you're perfect, the best. There will never be anyone better than you,' he said faithfully. 'I'll love you forever and make you happy all your life. Please believe me.'

'I still want you to think it over carefully,' I said. 'Marriage is a serious business, not a joking matter. It's for life.'

He was disappointed but tried to act as usual. I couldn't bear to see his upset face and tried to cheer him up. He gave me a smile. 'Don't worry about me, I won't give up. I believe I'll obtain your love by my faith.'

On returning to Melbourne, Dingda and I saw more of each other than before. No matter how often I warned myself not to accept him, to try to be rational; no matter how much I tried to keep him at a distance, our two hearts were getting closer. His sincerity, his thoughtfulness, his gentleness, his humour, his confidence and erudition were like invisible threads pulling me to him. He expressed his devotion to me in every aspect and I felt strongly his love for me, much deeper than with any of my previous boyfriends. When at last I believed completely that his love was genuine, I no longer worried about our age difference. I married him in Melbourne in early 1992.

The wedding was very simple as none of our parents or relatives could attend, only a few friends. We went to the Gold Coast for our honeymoon. Not even in my dreams had I ever thought I would marry in Australia, or marry a man so much younger than me. Sometimes I couldn't help thinking it was crazy – he had only been a primary-school boy when I had reached marriageable age – but our union must have been fated, I thought.

In April, soon after our honeymoon, it was time for me to return to China. I couldn't just forget about my career. Dingda was unwilling to let me go but he didn't stop me.

'I don't really want you to leave but I don't want our marriage to affect your career,' he said. 'I understand you and I respect your choice.'

The traditional Chinese belief that the husband always takes the lead in marriages, that the husband sings and the wife follows, had been handed down to my generation as well. A great many Chinese people still thought that the most important thing in a man's life was to have a successful career, and that the most important thing for a woman was to be a good daughter, wife and mother. Many women's careers or jobs were affected by their family situations: if anyone had to make sacrifices for the sake of the family, it would be the wife, not the husband. A lot of women thought this way too, and even those who didn't were often still the ones to make the sacrifice when faced with the choice. But though I wasn't prepared to sacrifice my career, I didn't think Dingda should come back to China – I couldn't ask him to give up his career for me. He had already been so understanding and supportive and I was so happy to have found such a sensible husband. I hadn't thought carefully about how we would solve the problem of living in different corners of the world, but it seemed that nothing was impossible as long as we loved each other.

So in late April, leaving Dingda alone, I went back to

China, with a new kind of worry and longing. There was no direct flight to Nanchang from Melbourne, and I had to get to Guangzhou first and then transfer to a domestic flight the following day. Ping and Hui flew to Guangzhou to meet me at the airport, and we sat up talking all night in our hotel, catching up on news after eighteen months away from each other.

Our flight didn't leave until five-thirty the next afternoon, so we had plenty of time to look around Guangzhou. I still needed to buy a few gifts, although I had bought some in Melbourne. It is a Chinese custom that people coming home after a long time away bring gifts to relatives and close friends. No matter how big or small, the gift is a sign of their regard.

As soon as I left the hotel with Ping and Hui, I felt dizzy from the stream of people, bicycles and vehicles. They came and went from all directions. What scared me the most was crossing the wide road. I couldn't see a traffic light nearby but people were crossing from everywhere. The vehicles showed no intention of stopping, just sounded their horns endlessly to alert whoever was in their way, and there was a constant ringing of bells by cyclists to warn pedestrians. I soon had a headache from the mix of noises, but Ping and Hui seemed to neither hear nor see anything and just kept walking among the crush of vehicles and bicycles. After crossing the road, Ping found I hadn't followed them. Like a coward, I still stood on the other side. I had been in traffic like this countless times before, but I had obviously become more used to the orderly flow of Australia than I realised.

In the stores, I found I could buy almost anything I

wanted, and much more cheaply than in Australia. Whenever we stopped to look at something, there would be at least one young lady walking up to patiently explain the product and its advantages, her face all smiles. This was a marked change in service manner, a manifestation of doing business with civility. I was pleased to see how much China was improving.

It was dark when we arrived home, but all the members of my family were waiting for us. I found my mother thinner and older. She pulled me nearer the light and said with tears on her face, 'Let me have a look at you.' Then she murmured, 'Good! Good! You look healthier.' She began to weep. 'You don't know how happy I was to hear you were getting married. Now your dead father and I don't worry about you any more.' Her words made me sorry for having delayed marriage for so long.

My mother and Jing had prepared a sumptuous dinner with more than ten dishes, and every one of them was my favourite. After dinner, my mother showed me my room, which had been newly furnished. She told me that although I had got married in Australia, she'd wanted to furnish this room as a bridal chamber. She also told me that, in accordance with traditional Chinese custom, on the day of my wedding my family had celebrated it at home, and let off a long string of two thousand firecrackers. I looked at my mother with deep gratitude but I couldn't get a single word out. That night, no one in my family went to bed until two o'clock.

After a few days' rest, I went to visit my colleagues at the court. Everyone was surprised at my sudden appearance. I told them I had married and asked Tu Ke to send wedding sweets to each office. President Geng and all my colleagues came to say hello, and I felt as if everything in the court was the same as before. But Tu Ke told me there had been big changes while I was away. Some people had retired and new young people had come in. All the staff in the court had been given a pay rise, and with annual awards and various allowances my income had increased by 500 per cent. I discovered that my sisters' and brothers-in-law's salaries had doubled. And although my mother had retired, because she'd been employed by a large private company she now received three times her previous salary in benefits. The general standard of living in Nanchang had risen a lot in that short space of time. A big shopping plaza had opened in the city, selling everything you could wish for, and there were more buses on the roads, so the traffic was less frantic.

A month later, I went to the Supreme Court in Beijing to report on my time in Australia. The leaders of the training centre were greatly concerned about my health, telling me not to rush to finish my graduation thesis but to pay attention to my wellbeing. They had already arranged with Beijing University for me to submit my thesis before the end of the year. I spent two weeks on further research in Beijing before going back to Nanchang, where I concentrated on writing my thesis.

But my thoughts often wandered. I couldn't help missing Dingda. I was surprised to see this change in myself, and understood at last the Chinese saying *yi ri san qiu*, meaning a day's separation can seem as long as three years. I also came to believe in the saying that a temporary parting will deepen love. Dingda and I had agreed to write to each other once a week, and that he would phone me once a week. As it turned out, he wrote two or three times a week, besides calling me. Our correspondence became the ambassador of our love, bringing our hearts even closer together. Anticipating, reading and answering his letters became important and happy events in my daily life, and if a letter was delayed even one day, it would make me anxious.

One evening, three months after I had left Melbourne, I sat waiting at the usual time for his call, but he didn't phone until late at night. I questioned him closely and he admitted he'd had an accident driving back home from the office. It was his fault, he said, because he wasn't concentrating on his driving but thinking about me. He told me not to worry as he was only hurt slightly. I didn't believe him and fretted about him every day. No matter how hard I tried to focus on my work, I couldn't stop missing him. I regretted that I couldn't fulfil my responsibility as a wife and look after him when he needed me. Finally, I decided to ask for leave to return to Australia.

President Geng did not have the authority to grant me this leave since it was for the purpose of going overseas; I needed to get permission from the personnel department. The previous minister had retired and the vice-minister had taken his place, and he had not forgotten the displeasure I had caused him when I applied to sit the examination for the training centre. Before I had finished explaining my situation, he interrupted and said coldly, 'You're married? Why didn't I know about it? Did you get permission from us?'

I showed him my marriage certificate and told him I had married in Australia.

He didn't even look at the certificate. 'I won't accept that. It's not legitimate.'

I pointed to the stamp of the Chinese consulate in Melbourne. 'Please have a look at this. It's been authorised by the Chinese consulate. It is legitimate.'

He waved his hand. 'I don't understand any of that. I only know you haven't applied for permission to marry from us, your work organisation.'

I tried to control myself and said patiently, 'Now is not the years of war. According to the marriage law, I need only apply for marriage in the marriage registration organisations.'

'There is a government document which says that if state officials wish to marry, they should get permission from their work organisation first,' he argued.

'Then please show me that document,' I said.

'I can't find it at the moment. Anyway, I remember it.'

I didn't want to continue this ridiculous argument as it was clear he was making things difficult for me on purpose. 'Then you won't authorise my leave to visit my husband?' I asked him.

'I don't acknowledge you have a husband.'

'But he's been hurt in an accident and needs my care.'

'That's not my business.'

I was too angry to talk any more and left his office full of grievances. That night, thinking about the minister's attitude, thinking of all the setbacks I'd faced in my career and in my love life, I felt very tired. I needed a rest; I needed a peaceful and happy family life. The more I thought about these things, the more I saw how important Dingda was to me, how important family life was to me. I told myself that we couldn't keep living in two countries like this. Whether it was in China or Australia, I wanted to live with my husband, like other women. Since I had already had success in my career, I felt I should try to be a good wife now, and to be a real woman. In China people still thought that women who only had a career were not real women, they could be real women only when they had a husband and children.

After some days of serious consideration, I decided to resign, although I understood what this meant and the price I would pay. But I believed Dingda would compensate me with his true love; he wouldn't let me regret this decision some day in the future.

My mother was sorry to hear I would have to give up my career, but she fully understood my decision. 'I know how hard it is for you to choose between your work and family,' she said, 'but you've paid a lot for pursuing your career, and you haven't had a family until now. I can't say I think it's wrong for you to give up your work for your personal life this time. You're married now – it's not good for you two to live separately for too long. And leaving the Railway Court doesn't mean your career is ended. Gold always shines, wherever it is. You can start a new career in a new place.'

My sisters and colleagues also supported my decision. They said, 'You shouldn't have come back at all. How can you live separately once you're married?' 'You can develop your career in Australia.' 'You've already been successful in your career. As a woman, you should regard your family as the most important thing now.'

And so I, who had never imagined that love could have such great magical power, and had certainly never thought it could make me give up my beloved career, finally submitted my resignation in September 1992 and went back to Melbourne to be with Dingda. I had ended a period of extraordinary years and was now starting a new phase of my life journey. Deep down, I did not think this turn of events was strange as I knew I had grass fortune and that my life in Australia would prove no less extraordinary – grass, after all, is stronger than flowers, even though it is less beautiful. As the poem says, even a raging fire can not burn the grass down, it shoots up again when the spring breeze blows.

Also available from Penguin Books

FALLING LEAVES
THE TRUE STORY OF AN UNWANTED CHINESE DAUGHTER

Adeline Yen Mah

Her grand aunt formed the Shanghai Women's Bank. Her father was known as the miracle boy with the power of turning iron into gold. Yet in this affluent Chinese family the fifth child and youngest daughter, Adeline, suffered appalling emotional abuse.

Set against the background of changing political times and the collision of East and West, *Falling Leaves* describes how, despite the legacy of her painful childhood, Adeline Yen Mah survived to make a successful career. Told with all the suspense and emotional force of a novel, this true story is moving in its eloquent simplicity and, through the dignity of its indomitable protagonist, finally uplifting.

'*Charged with emotion. Adeline Yen Mah has laid bare her painful family story. A vivid portrait of the human capacity for meanness, malice – and love.*'

Jung Chang

'*Brilliant, compelling and unforgettable ... A heart-rending modern-day Cinderella story set against the turbulence of twentieth-century China.*'
Nien Cheng, author of Life and Death in Shanghai

'*An honest and memorable book. I was gripped from beginning to end.*'
Lynn Pan, author of Tracing it Home
and Sons of the Yellow Emperor

CHINESE CINDERELLA
THE SECRET STORY OF AN UNWANTED CHINESE DAUGHTER

Adeline Yen Mah

'Tell me what my real mama looked like. I can't picture her face.' 'There are no photographs of her,' said Aunt Baba ... 'Your father ordered all photographs destroyed.'

When Adeline Yen Mah's mother died giving birth to her, the family considered Adeline bad luck and she was made to feel unwanted all her life. *Chinese Cinderella* is the story of her struggle for acceptance and how she overcame the odds to prove her worth.

Following the success of the critically acclaimed, international bestseller *Falling Leaves, Chinese Cinderella* is a true and moving account of Adeline's childhood up to the age of fourteen. It is an unforgettable story.

PIECES OF BLUE
Kerry McGinnis

At the age of six Kerry McGinnis loses her mother. Her father, left with four young children to raise, gathers up his family and leaves the city to go droving. For the next fifteen years the McGinnis clan travels the continent, droving, horse-breaking and living off the land. Schoolrooms, comfort and civilisation are a long way off as Kerry grows up in the harsh outback, where animals are her closest friends. With the memory of her absent mother ever present, Kerry begins her difficult journey to young womanhood.

'Kerry McGinnis's personal – and personable – story offers insights into an Australia unknown by urbanites. And into the human values and verities that underwrite life there.'

The Australian

'It is the author's word pictures of the sights, smells and sounds of the bush, and her perceptive rendering of the characters along the way, that make Pieces of Blue *a book to be treasured.*'

Sunshine Coast Sunday

Pieces of Blue also has a compelling sequel in *Heart Country*.